AT HIS FEET
with Encouragement Café

Devotional Journal

This world is not our home. Life can deliver some hard blows and difficult times. Even during our highest highs we are faced with the realization that we are flawed. These daily scriptures and devotions have been written to encourage and breathe fresh hope into your life.

We pray that these scriptures and powerful little devotions will inspire you to spend time with Jesus. Be encouraged to look for Him, talk to Him, and listen to Him. Grasp how wide and long and high and deep His love is.

Visit us often at www.EncouragementCafe.com.

May our Lord Jesus Christ Himself and God our Father, who loved us and by His grace gave us eternal encouragement and good hope, encourage your hearts and strengthen you in every good deed and word.

2 Thessalonians 2:16,17 NIV

These contributing authors are all a part of the Encouragement Café Team:
Brenda Bearden, Dana Cline, Carol Davis, Ramona Davis, Stephanie Davis, Noelle Dey, Jennifer Donaldson, Glenn Edwards, Judy Fussell, Debbie Giese, Dale Hancock, Weeta Heath, Allison Herrin, Andrea Hine, Michelle Axton Kelly, Britta Lafont, Michelle Lazurek, Annah Matthews, Lee Merrill, Dawn Neely, Dallas Paetzold, Paris Paetzold, Savannah Parvu, Luann Prater, MaryKay Rath, Amanda and Michael Ryals, Betty Shoopman, Kathy and Will Sweeny, Wendi Westmoreland, Jamy Whitaker, Tiffany Williams and Debbie Williard.
Cover design & artwork by Betty Shoopman (www.BettyShoopman.com)
Blessings,
The Encouragement Café Team

Press on

Not that I have already obtained all this, or have already been made perfect, but I press on to take hold of that for which Christ Jesus took hold of me.
Philippians 3:12 NIV 1984

Pressure cookers rattle, sizzle, and squeal as they allow only the smallest bit of steam to escape producing tender morsels that melt in your mouth. Life presses in on me until I rattle, sizzle and squeal, but God reminds me to press on, He isn't finished with me yet. Maybe the steam is seeping out of your life too. Friend, breathe! God is producing in you a tender heart.

1

Hope

Find rest, O my soul, in God alone;
my hope comes from Him.
Psalm 62:5 NIV 1984

The restoration your soul requires is not the same as being physically refreshed. When the soul is weary everything about life becomes dull, hard to face. To have hope is essential and foundational to facing life in this fallen world. The author of this verse knows his soul can only gain hope from God alone. God's promises, His faithfulness, are proven and life giving. God is the definition of goodness, mercy and love. Knowing Him alone brings your soul rest.

_____

_____

_____

_____

_____

_____

_____

_____

_____

_____

_____

_____

_____

_____

_____

_____

_____

2

Identified

And now you Gentiles have also heard the truth, the Good News that God saves you. And when you believed in Christ, He identified you as His own by giving you the Holy Spirit, whom He promised long ago.
Ephesians 1:13 NLT

Recognizing we cannot go it alone is just where we need to be for His love to begin to change us. Good news indeed! God sent His Son to conquer the grave and didn't stop there. He identified us as His own for good! You have not been left alone. You are identified by Him who knows us all as His by the Holy Spirit within us.

3

Journaling

Then the LORD replied: "Write down the revelation and make it plain on tablets so that a herald may run with it."
Habakkuk 2:2 NIV

How often do we argue with God over something that seems unjust? When bad things happen to good people, we say, "Why, God?" Sometimes evil prevails, just as in the story of Habakkuk, but never fear. God had a plan in 605 B.C., He has a plan now. When we journal our thoughts and prayers we can look back in two weeks or two years and see how God brought us through a crisis and grew our faith beyond measure. Sharing our own revelations with others is a testament to God's faithfulness. Write it down and run with it so He may be exalted in all things.

_____

_____

_____

_____

_____

_____

_____

_____

_____

_____

_____

_____

_____

_____

_____

_____

_____

4

Forgiven

Therefore, I tell you, her many sins have been forgiven —
for she loved much.
But he who has been forgiven little loves little.
Luke 7:47 NIV 1984

In Christ Jesus you have been forgiven! In gratitude go and love
much, showing God's mercy to the lost.
When you share His great love, you will be blessed and be a blessing
to others for the glory of God.

_____

5

Determination

But Daniel determined that he would not defile himself…
Daniel 1:8 MSG

The entire Old Testament book of Daniel and the grand adventures of
Shadrach, Meshach and Abednego, probably would never have taken
place without this brave young man, Daniel, making up his mind
ahead of time that he would not defile himself. Because he purposed
in his heart that he would be obedient to God's law and
do things God's way, he became a great man of God.
Let's be determined to obey God's Word and live our lives His way,
as we embark on the great journey to come.

6

Received

*You're no longer strangers or outsiders. You **belong** here, with as much right to the name Christian as anyone.*
Ephesians 2:19 MSG

Periods of loneliness fill a good part of our lives. But when we receive Christ Jesus, our Protector, He accepts us. I found this to be true during middle school, where there were many days of isolation, no one to talk to but God. He will listen. Not only does He listen, He loves. He receives us for who we are, in spite of everything we have done and will do. He is our Friend, our Daddy.

7

Praiseworthy

*Through Jesus, therefore, let us continually offer to God a
sacrifice of praise—the fruit of lips that confess His name.
Hebrews 13:15 NIV 1984*

God is able to renew our minds and hearts in any circumstance.
In the darkest depths of our souls, He knows us and yet still loves us.
That alone gives us reason to praise Him in every situation. Through
Jesus, we may boldly approach God's throne without hesitation;
without condemnation and without fear, to lift our praises to Him.

8

Beloved

No one who is born of God will continue to sin,
because God's seed remains in him;
he cannot go on sinning, because he has been born of God.
1 John 3:9 NIV 1984

If you love God and have asked Him into your heart and to forgive
you of your sins then He will always be with you. You will never again
be alone. You will continue to sin but not make a practice of it.
You will strive to be like Christ and the Holy Spirit will be there to
help you do this. You are His beloved.

_____

_____

_____

_____

_____

_____

_____

_____

_____

_____

_____

_____

_____

_____

_____

_____

9

Belief

Now faith is the substance of things hoped for,
the evidence of things not seen.
Hebrews 11:1 KJV

What is the enemy of belief? It is knowledge in the form of proof.
We know that ignorance is NOT bliss and we should grow in
knowledge and wisdom. However, proof will never convince those
who do not first choose to believe. This is why we call it faith.
Don't let the lie of proof prevent you from seeing truth.
Sometimes you have to believe in order to see.

_____

_____

_____

_____

_____

_____

_____

_____

_____

_____

_____

_____

_____

_____

_____

_____

_____

_____

10

Sufficiency

All Scripture is God-breathed and is useful for teaching,
rebuking, correcting and training in righteousness,
so that the man of God may be thoroughly equipped
for every good work.
2 Timothy 3:16-17 NIV 1984

God's Word has all the answers. Sure we always see His Word as our source of spiritual knowledge. Let's not forget that it's also practical. From it you can learn how to deal with money, fear, children, spouses, the poor, etc. If you have a problem, He is the answer. Nothing is too big for our God. His Word will suffice.

11

Courageous

Have I not commanded you? Be strong and courageous.
Do not be terrified; do not be discouraged, for the LORD
your God will be with you wherever you go.
Joshua 1:9 NIV 1984

When the troubles of this world overtake you and leave you filled
with feelings of fear and isolation, remember you are not alone. You
can courageously walk through any trial knowing the LORD your God
is with you wherever you go.

_____

_____

_____

_____

_____

_____

_____

_____

_____

_____

_____

_____

_____

_____

_____

_____

_____

_____

12

Happiness

*Happy **is he** that **has** the God of Jacob for his help,*
*Whose hope **is** in the LORD his God.*
Psalm 146:5 NKJV

Somewhere along the way, we have come to the idea that God's business is to make us happy. We pray for things that we believe will make our lives happy, comfortable and perfect. When we choose to focus on God and what He wants to do in us and through us, that is when true happiness, deep and abiding joy, is ours!

_____

_____

_____

_____

_____

_____

_____

_____

_____

_____

_____

_____

_____

_____

_____

_____

_____

_____

13

Barnabas

Joseph, a Levite from Cyprus, whom the apostles called Barnabas (which means son of encouragement)...
Acts 4:36 NIV

Joseph of Cyprus became Barnabas! He was a man who experienced a name change because of his character. His passion was to spur on early Christians to bring God greater glory. His name change was not self-ordained. The people he influenced were responsible for tagging this man with a higher, more noble moniker. Barnabas was a man who became great by lifting others up. Someone in your life could use a "Barnabas-like" effort from you today.
Allow God to spread His encouraging love through you.

14

Flow

Above all else, guard your heart,
for everything you do flows from it.
Proverbs 4:23 NIV

Your heart is the core of your being. From a health matter,
everything does flow from it. However wherever your heart is,
your actions will flow from that. Are you guarding your heart
to only what is beneficial and godly?

_____

_____

_____

_____

_____

_____

_____

_____

_____

_____

_____

_____

_____

_____

_____

_____

_____

15

Cry

Listen to my prayer, O God, do not ignore my plea;
hear me and answer me. My thoughts trouble me and I am
distraught because of what my enemy is saying,
because of the threats of the wicked...
Psalm 55:1-3 NIV

Our prayer and cry for help should be to God alone. Yet, so often, I spend so much of my time crying out to friends, family members or co-workers. Nothing changes. Oh, I may feel better just for getting it off my chest; but pretty soon, my thoughts turn in the wrong direction and I am back at square one. The enemy then chimes in and begins to tell me every lie that he thinks I will believe. Maybe today is one of those days when you need to stop crying out to all of those around you and start crying out to the One who knows your heart and can see the bigger picture. He loves you. Your cry for help is a sweet sound to your Savior.

_____

_____

_____

_____

_____

_____

_____

_____

_____

_____

_____

_____

16

Content

*Let **your** conduct **be** without covetousness;*
be content with such things as you have.
For He Himself has said, "I will never leave you
nor forsake you."
Hebrews 13:5 NKJV

It is good for us to see our need for God. The less we have, the more we can see that need. "The Joneses" are searching just like the rest of us; though it may be more difficult for them, for they are not aware of any immediate needs that God is fulfilling. Use your current circumstances to draw close to God. Allow Him to provide for you, so that the contentedness that goes beyond material wealth can truly satisfy your soul. A content heart acts in love, represents God, and so touches the heart of God.

_____
_____
_____
_____
_____
_____
_____
_____
_____
_____
_____
_____
_____
_____

Redeemed

Fear not, for I have redeemed you;
I have summoned you by name; you are Mine.
Isaiah 43:1b NIV 1984

The God of the universe loves us. He knows us by name. He is with us wherever we go. We can trust fully that when we cry out to Him for help He will hear our cry and answer. He only requires that we come to Him in complete surrender, trusting that He has everything we need. Yes, Jesus loves me. Yes, Jesus loves me. Yes Jesus loves me, the Bible tells me so.

_____
_____
_____
_____
_____
_____
_____
_____
_____
_____
_____
_____
_____
_____
_____
_____
_____
_____

Trust

Trust in the LORD with all your heart and lean not on your own understanding.
Proverbs 3:5 NIV

Why do we often feel as though we have to figure everything out? While taking care of my mother-in-law, there were so very many distractions; it seemed EVERYone was trying to figure out the next step. Instead, Jesus kept speaking softly to my heart: don't try to understand... I am working... just trust Me completely. It is a difficult concept for me, complete trust. Not occasional, not circumstantial, not humanly understood. Just trust.

Lord, please grow my faith to trust You – completely.

19

Trials Build Character

For everyone will be tested with fire. Salt is good for seasoning. But if it loses its flavor, how do you make it salty again? You must have the qualities of salt among yourselves and live in peace with each other.
Mark 9:49-50 NLT

Whenever you feel like you are enduring something that you just can't seem to make it through, have you ever considered that it might just be for a purpose? At some point you will go through the "fire." Through it He refines our character and we become priceless possessions to be used for His glory! We become the salt of the earth and the light of the world! Will you trust Him through the challenge?

_____

_____

_____

_____

_____

_____

_____

_____

_____

_____

_____

_____

_____

_____

_____

20

Piece by Piece

But the things that come out of a person's mouth
come from the heart, and these defile them.
Matthew 15:18 NIV

The words that come from our mouth speak about the condition of
our hearts. We are deceived into believing we have all our pain and
hurt buried deep. What flows out of a contaminated and polluted
heart? Negativity and criticism. Bitterness and resentment.
God is the Great Physician and He wants to heal our hearts.
If we will allow Him, He will remove all that debris, piece by piece.
The change is evident when He creates a new heart in us.

God is in the Midst

God is in the midst of her, she shall not be moved;
God shall help her, just at the break of dawn.
Psalm 46:5 NKJV

In the early morning hours, do you wonder how you will face the day
or complete all the tasks the lie ahead? Remember that God is in your
midst and He is with you. He is here to help you face the tasks of
today and accomplish the good works set before you.
Firmly plant yourself in His Hands today.

22

Enough

Therefore, if anyone is in Christ, he is a new creation.
The old has passed away; behold, the new has come.
2 Corinthians 5:17 ESV

YOU are a new creation. You sin, but you are not called "sinner." You are not called by that name. YOU are redeemed. YOU are beloved. YOU are adopted. When you get that stuck feeling, the feeling that you are not good enough... and might never get there... just remember that the sacrifice of Christ is enough.

23

Standing on Solid Ground

…He set my feet on a rock
and gave me a firm place to stand.
Psalm 40:2 NIV

When I was nine years old I almost drowned at the city pool.
While struggling to reach the nearest ladder, I couldn't fight my
fatigue. When panic set in, I began to sink. Suddenly, strong arms
grabbed me around my waist and lifted me to safety. I never knew the
name of the lifeguard.

But I know the name of the One who placed my feet on solid ground
and rescued me from a life of defeat. Jesus is His name and I thank
Him every day for His rescue! Have you thanked Him today?

24

Hope

O Israel, hope in the LORD!
For with the LORD there is steadfast love,
and with Him is great power to redeem.
Psalm 130:7 NRSV

I get so wrapped up sometimes wishing people would change and grow a little faster. Not necessarily for their own benefit either, but to make my life easier. Can you relate? Then I remember that God is the only One I should put my hope in, and that when it looks like all is lost, He is able to redeem every situation.

Instead of worrying, trust in Him. He's got it covered.

_____
_____
_____
_____
_____
_____
_____
_____
_____
_____
_____
_____
_____
_____
_____
_____
_____
_____

A Bad Habit

With the tongue we praise our Lord and Father,
and with it we curse human beings, who have been made
in God's likeness. Out of the same mouth come praise and
cursing. My brothers and sisters, this should not be.
Can both fresh water and salt water flow from the same
spring? My brothers and sisters, can a fig tree bear olives,
or a grapevine bear figs?
Neither can a salt spring produce fresh water.
James 3:9-12 NIV

What comes from the mouth... comes from the heart.
By spewing out hurtful or mean talk from our lips about someone...
it is not only a bad habit, but SIN.

Fear Not

Do not fear, for I have redeemed you;
I have summoned you by name; you are Mine.
Isaiah 43:1b NIV

"Do not fear" really hits me. I know that within the Bible, God commands us not to fear over 365 times. That is one for every day of the year and extra for those difficult days. Therefore, it must be really important to God. He wants us to know that we do not have to fear because He promises to be with us.

27

Love

Give thanks to the LORD, for He is good;
His love endures forever.
Psalm 118:1 NIV

Human love is but a mere shadow of God's love. This perfect love
drives out fear. There is no condemnation. His love envelops and
brings peace that passes understanding. God's love never ends. He is
love. Sin has been removed so we can receive this love of perfection.
Receive! Bask in it! Rejoice that you are loved in a far greater way
than you can even comprehend.

28

He Knows Your Name

… Do not fear, for I have redeemed you;
I have summoned you by name; you are Mine.
Isaiah 43:1 NIV

Friend, is your heart flailing and fretting over keeping everyone in your life happy? Exhausting, isn't it? It's time to give your heart a rest. Why not spend some time meditating on this truth: whether the world applauds your efforts or not, your Savior knows your name, and He forever claims you as His. Feel better?

Friend Me

A man of too many friends comes to ruin,
but there is a Friend who sticks closer than a brother.
Proverbs 18:24 NASB

God, thank You for showing us how to be a true friend in this world of superficial connections and hectic schedules. Reveal to us those You have placed in our lives. Grant us the courage to get in the trenches with them as we live our lives together. Help us share our hearts in celebrations, illnesses, new beginnings, mourning, filling needs, providing grace and laughter. May we always remember to be the friend we want to receive.

30

Discipline

Endure hardship as discipline;
God is treating you as His children.
For what children are not disciplined by their father?
Hebrews 12:7 NIV

When trials come your way, do you feel abandoned and neglected
by God? Do you feel like God doesn't love you? Take heart! God is
using those trials to rid the undesirable things in your life and produce
within you the fruits of His Spirit. What trials are you facing right
now that God might be using for your benefit? What fruit might be
produced as a result of these trials?

31

Sent

Again He said, "Peace be with you.
As the Father has sent Me, so I am sending you."
John 20:21 NLT

God sent Jesus on a mission. Jesus was sent to be a sacrifice.
He came to breathe life into hopeless situations. He served. He loved
the unlovable. God sent His Son, and likewise Jesus turns and hands
the torch to you and me. He is sending us to be a living sacrifice and
to breathe new life into tired hearts. He is sending us to serve and to
love the unlovable. Jesus is sending you today, friend.

Transforming Your Mind

Do not conform to the pattern of this world,
but be transformed by the renewing of your mind.
Then you will be able to test and approve what
God's will is—His good, pleasing and perfect will.
Romans 12:2 NIV

When we surrender our lives to the Lord we are to be set apart from the world. We are no longer supposed to walk, speak and act like the world. We are to speak the truth and act in a way that is pleasing to the Lord. We must transform our minds by changing our thinking. Our thoughts fuel our feelings and our feelings fuel our actions.

33

Weathering the Storm

*... do not be afraid of those who kill the body and
after that have no more that they can do.*
Luke 12:4 NASB

Dreading the price He would pay for our punishment,
Jesus begged the Father to allow His God-given purpose to pass by.
However, rather than letting fear dictate His decision,
Jesus chose to trust the Father's promises and offered His body over
to pursue God's will. Are there storms in your life that are paralyzing
you with fear? Trust in His promises and look for the rainbows
He places in the midst of your storms.

34

sku-ba-la

...I consider them rubbish, that I may gain Christ.
Philippians 3:8 NIV 1984

The Greek word for 'rubbish' is pronounced 'sku-ba-la.' So the probing question in my heart today is: As I look around my life and see all the 'things' we have accumulated; all the relationships we have fostered; all the prizes we have attained, would I consider it all 'sku-ba-la' in comparison to knowing...
I mean REALLY knowing Christ?
What are you running hard after today?

_____

_____

_____

_____

_____

_____

_____

_____

_____

_____

_____

_____

_____

_____

_____

_____

_____

_____

_____

Never

No one will be able to stand up against you all the days of your life. As I was with Moses, so I will be with you; I will never leave you nor forsake you.
Joshua 1:5 NIV 1984

This promise would be hollow if we did not know how God was "with" Moses. History proves how God counseled, guided, protected, and prospered Moses. He literally never left Moses throughout his entire life on earth. This same promise extends to you.
You never have to be fearful of what tomorrow, or next year, holds when God is with you.

_____

_____

_____

_____

_____

_____

_____

_____

_____

_____

_____

_____

_____

_____

_____

_____

Genuine

Love each other with genuine affection,
and take delight in honoring each other.
Romans 12:10 NLT

Giving others our attention is showing God's love. The world sees passing glances and knows them for what they are. See your world through His eyes today. Look for those who He wants to love through you. Today is a new opportunity to give of yourself for His glory. Take delight in His true and genuine affection toward you and pass it on.

37

The Gate

I tell you the truth, I am the gate for the sheep.
John 10:7 NIV 1984

Gates have always intrigued me. They either keep something in or something out and when they are left open, their intent is lost. In John 10 we are reminded of the gate that was used to keep the sheep secure on summer nights. A makeshift corral was constructed with a simple opening. At night the shepherd lay down across the entrance making him the gate. Jesus Himself is both the Shepherd and the only gate into the Kingdom of God. How reassuring that as our Shepherd, Jesus knows each of us by name, He leads us to new pastures and He goes ahead of us to make our paths smooth. He lay down His life for us so that one day we may enter the gates of heaven. Thank You, Lord!

_____

_____

_____

_____

_____

_____

_____

_____

_____

_____

_____

_____

_____

_____

_____

_____

_____

38

Covered

Therefore He is able to save completely those who come to God through Him, because He always lives to intercede for them.
Hebrews 7:25 NIV

Just remember today that whatever failures or whatever storm you are in right now, you have a Savior in Christ Jesus who is always praying for you. Be encouraged beloved you are covered in prayer by our High Priest, Jesus!

39

Stuff

The LORD gave and the LORD has taken away.
Blessed be the name of the LORD.
Job 1:21b NASB

A few years ago, we were forced to evacuate for a hurricane. It was terrible trying to decide between what was most important to take and what to leave. With a few family heirlooms, some irreplaceable photos, and our baby tucked safely in our car,
we closed the door to our home and my husband spoke this verse.
It instantly reminded me that it was all just stuff.
Our greatest possession, Jesus, would sustain us through the storm.

_____

_____

_____

_____

_____

_____

_____

_____

_____

_____

_____

_____

_____

_____

_____

Intertwined

And this is my prayer: that your love may abound more and more in knowledge and depth of insight, so that you may be able to discern what is best and may be pure and blameless until the day of Christ, filled with the fruit of righteousness that comes through Jesus Christ —
to the glory and praise of God.
Philippians 1:9-11 NIV 1984

Our love is not merely a feeling, but is based on what Christ has done for us. As we spend time with God, studying His Word, our hearts and minds grow together. Our hearts become intertwined with His.

_____

_____

_____

_____

_____

_____

_____

_____

_____

_____

_____

_____

_____

_____

_____

_____

Illuminated

But we have this treasure in jars of clay
to show that this all-surpassing power is from God
and not from us.
2 Corinthians 4:7 NIV

How bright can you shine? We often lose sight of how we fit into
God's plans. Does a light bulb shine when it's in the box?
No, it must be plugged into a power source. God spoke light into
existence and He created you as a clay chalice through which the
Holy Spirit can be poured out into this very dark world.

Faithful

... for His compassions never fail. They are new every morning; great is Your faithfulness. I say to myself, "The LORD is my portion; therefore I will wait for Him."
Lamentations 3:22-24 NIV

The same compassion the LORD had for the Israelites, who were wandering in the desert, is the same compassion He has for you. He faithfully provided the perfect portion of Manna, to meet their needs. He is your Perfect Portion. Just as the Israelites had to wait upon Him to receive the promised land, you too have been given the promise of a place He is preparing.

43

Enabling

It is God who arms me with strength and makes my way perfect. He makes my feet like the feet of a deer; He enables me to stand on the heights. He trains my hands for battle; my arms can bend a bow of bronze.
Psalm 18:32-34 NIV 1984

The beauty and encouragement of this verse comes from sharing the author's realizations of how uniquely the LORD has blessed him. God perfectly and intentionally equips you for each battle you face. Your abilities will be beyond your belief just as God is beyond our comprehension.

_____

_____

_____

_____

_____

_____

_____

_____

_____

_____

_____

_____

_____

_____

_____

Wisdom

The beginning of wisdom is this: Get wisdom.
Though it cost all you have, get understanding.
Proverbs 4:7 NIV

The words "I don't know" are muttered so often in a humble way.
There is a lot that we do not know here on earth. Though we are
still learning, there is so much wisdom that we have not yet obtained.
Digging into the Word is our hope of gaining that wisdom. If you're
anything like me, you struggle in this area. What can we change in our
everyday actions to make getting wisdom more of a priority?

_____

_____

_____

_____

_____

_____

_____

_____

_____

_____

_____

_____

_____

_____

_____

_____

_____

Surgery

For the Word of God is alive and active.
Sharper than any double-edged sword, it penetrates even to
dividing soul and spirit, joints and marrow;
it judges the thoughts and attitudes of the heart.
Hebrews 4:12 NIV

God's Word works to perform spiritual surgery to remove and repair
those things that need attention. I can act in a certain manner and fool
most people, but God's Word penetrates into the deepest parts
of my heart and reveals my motives and my attitudes.
That's one reason we avoid God's Word… because we realize it can
see right through us. Take time to let God's Word perform
the spiritual surgery that will make you whole!

Dad

When my father and my mother forsake me,
then the LORD will take care of me.
Psalm 27:10 NKJV

Being a parent is tough. There's no map, blow-by-blow instruction manual, or heavenly trainer motivating and directing their every decision. They are bound to do things that therapists will later condemn. We can blame them for abandoning us. Or we can accept their humanity, the fact that we have zero control over them, and instead go to the Father that is with us every second. He did, after all, create us, bless us, watch us all of our days, and promise us the security of His presence and fortitude at any moment we ask for it.
So ask your Dad. He's listening.

47

Majestic

O LORD, our Lord, how majestic is your name in all the earth! ...When I consider Your heavens, the work of Your fingers, the moon and the stars, which You have set in place, what is man that You are mindful of him, the son of man that You care for him?
Psalm 8:1,3-4 NIV 1984

Our Heavenly Father created a beautiful world. You can see His Majesty in the skies, oceans, mountains and every living thing. Yet, despite all these things, He counts man as His greatest creation. The Creator of the universe desires a relationship with you, His child.

_____

_____

_____

_____

_____

_____

_____

_____

_____

_____

_____

_____

_____

_____

_____

_____

_____

48

Victorious

I have told you these things, so that in Me you may have peace. In this world you will have trouble.
But take heart! I have overcome the world.
John 16:33 NIV

Thank You, Jesus, for reminding us that You have already won the ultimate victory! So, even in the most troublesome times, when we are most distraught and downtrodden, we can claim the only true peace — that which is found in YOU, our Victorious Savior!

<hr>

49

Sanctified

May God Himself, the God of peace, sanctify you through and through. May your whole spirit, soul and body be kept blameless at the coming of our Lord Jesus Christ. The One who calls you is faithful and He will do it.
1 Thessalonians 5:23-24 NIV

Sometimes we try so hard to be the "Perfect Christian" when in fact there is no such thing. You will wear yourself out trying. Stop, take a deep breath and relax. Be yourself and let Him shine through you. He lives in you, He is faithful and He will do it.

_____

_____

_____

_____

_____

_____

_____

_____

_____

_____

_____

_____

_____

_____

50

Focus

... "Teacher, I brought my son so you could heal him.
He is possessed by an evil spirit that won't let him talk."
The father instantly cried out, "I do believe, but help me
overcome my unbelief!"
Mark 9:17, 24 NLT

This father had been focused on his child's problem for so long. Then he met Jesus! He turned his focus away from the situation and onto Jesus and his son was delivered. What situation are you facing today that seems insufferable? Turn your focus to Jesus and His promises and you too can be delivered. He is faithful even in the most unbearable of situations!

51

Spirit-Filled Heart

The human heart is the most deceitful of all things, and desperately wicked. Who really knows how bad it is?
Jeremiah 17:9 NLT

Jeremiah received these words from the Lord.
God did not create our hearts this way; it is a result of the fall of man. Our hearts are more deceitful than any other creation, including Satan himself! When God sends someone to speak His Truth into our hearts, we see our hearts for what they are, and we allow the Spirit to transform our hearts.
A Spirit-filled heart is the heart God created for us to have.

52

Protection and Strength

The LORD is my strength and my shield;
My heart trusted in Him, and I am helped;
Therefore my heart greatly rejoices,
And with my song I will praise Him.
Psalm 28:7 NKJV

Your heart can choose to trust in a lot of things but the Lord is your strength and shield. Praise Him today and rejoice that you can place your heart in His Hands and receive protection, strength, and help from Him.

53

Abide

I am the vine; you are the branches.
If you remain in Me, and I in you, you will bear much fruit;
apart from Me you can do nothing.
John 15:5 NIV

Abide.
Not strive.
Not wrestle, with a tight chest and an anxious heart.
Not. Come. Up. Short.
Abide.
Inhale. Exhale.
Live there.
Be settled. Accept, with peace.
Remain, at rest.

Help

*Because He Himself suffered when He was tempted,
He is able to help those who are being tempted.
Hebrews 2:18 NIV*

It is easy to believe that Jesus found temptation easier to deal with than that which we experience. This verse refutes that notion. Jesus suffered when He was tempted and by that suffering can intimately relate with our struggles with temptation. He knows the tug-of-war, the anxiety, the feeling of helplessness we face in our weakness. In those times He offers His strength, His armor against the attack, His assurance that we face nothing He has not already conquered.

A Reason to Sing

I will sing of the LORD'S great love forever...
Psalm 89:1 NIV

The Lord has taken away the fear of death. He has freed us from sin and we are forgiven, past, present and future. In our weakness, His strength is made perfect. His precious thoughts toward us are more than the grains of sand. He who knows us best loves us most. The Lord is preparing a place for us and one day we will see Him face to face. We are invited to supper at a table that He will prepare. That is a reason to sing!

Plans

For whoever wishes to save his life will lose it;
but whoever loses his life for My sake will find it.
Matthew 16:25 NASB

I knew exactly what I wanted. I knew what I wanted my life to look like. I knew it all. I knew it right up until the minute I knew I was wrong. The day I gave up what I thought I was supposed to have, is the day I found my life. Trading our agendas for God's plan is scary business, but it is the only way to live fully in Him.

_____

_____

_____

_____

_____

_____

_____

_____

_____

_____

_____

_____

_____

_____

_____

_____

_____

_____

57

Rejoice

This is the day the Lord has made;
We will rejoice and be glad in it.
Psalm 118:24 NKJV

Each day brings on pressures of work, school, family, appointments...
the list goes on and on and on. But each day there is a reason to
REJOICE. Take the time each day to find those precious moments
that you can REJOICE IN THE LORD...
it does the heart, mind and soul good!

Seek First

But seek first His kingdom and His righteousness...
Matthew 6:33 NIV

"But seek first His kingdom" plainly tells us to turn to God first. He needs to be our first choice and not our last resort. We are called to seek Him first. God demands first place in our lives. The word "seek" means "to pursue, crave." The next portion, "and His righteousness" is talking about being filled with God's desires and willing to serve and obey Him in everything. The question we have to ask ourselves is "what is really important?"

_____

_____

_____

_____

_____

_____

_____

_____

_____

_____

_____

_____

_____

_____

_____

_____

_____

59

Voices

My sheep listen to My voice; I know them,
and they follow Me.
John 10:27 NIV

Let the wise listen and add to their learning...
Proverbs 1:5 NIV

So many voices from the world are screaming. They scramble our
vision and can lead us astray. Christ is gentle and humble in heart.
He is our Creator and knows us inside and out. He knows our needs
and what satisfies. Follow Him. He will lead you to safe pastures.
Peace is the result. His peace He will give you.
Still your mind. Seek Him. He will be found.

Hand-made Heart

He made their hearts,
so He understands everything they do.
Psalm 33:15 NLT

'm not much of a crafter. My creative ideas never seem to turn out
quite right. Did you know God's a Master Crafter?
With His tender hands and heart, He fashions each of us into just
who He wants us to be. He knows we aren't perfect,
and nothing we do takes Him by surprise.
He understands us like only a Creator God can.

61

Sparkle

Finally, brothers and sisters, whatever is true,
whatever is noble, whatever is right, whatever is pure,
whatever is lovely, whatever is admirable — if anything is
excellent or praiseworthy — think about such things.
Philippians 4:8 NIV

It is easy to become entangled in our world's polluted thoughts.
Television, news reports, office gossip and much more compete for
our attention. Often we find our hearts stuck within dirty, sin filled
streets. Today, step out with the intention of letting your heart be pure.
Keep ugliness out and may a ray of Christ's brilliant sparkle
encourage you and those around you.

Cultivating Your Soil

"For three years now I've been coming to look for fruit on this fig tree and haven't found any. Cut it down! Why should it use up the soil?" "Sir," the man replied, "leave it alone for one more year, and I'll dig around it and fertilize it. If it bears fruit next year, fine! If not, then cut it down."
Luke 13:7-9 NIV

God sees the potential in us, even when others don't see it.
He knows fruit is produced through cultivating the soil and
is willing to put the time and effort into doing so.
How can you cultivate your soil today?

_____

_____

_____

_____

_____

_____

_____

_____

_____

_____

_____

_____

_____

_____

_____

_____

63

Laughter

A cheerful heart is good medicine,
but a broken spirit saps a person's strength.
Proverbs 17:22 NLT

Looking in the mirror after a long day at work, I found a very green piece of spinach in my front two teeth. All the people I spoke with ran through my mind. I was mortified. Although laughter was not my first reaction, when I finally gave in, it was truly medicine to my soul. Do you feel sapped of strength? When we take ourselves too seriously, we get exhausted. Let's lighten up and laugh more!

Living for Christ

I have been crucified with Christ and I no longer live,
but Christ lives in me. The life I now live in the body,
I live by faith in the Son of God,
who loved me and gave Himself for me.
Galatians 2:20 NIV

When we accept Christ as our personal Lord and Savior,
His Spirit comes to dwell inside of us.
We stop living for ourselves and start living for the Lord.
We are to think of our bodies as the temples of the Lord.

65

Achieving Real Success

… present your bodies a living sacrifice
… do not be conformed to this world
… be transformed by the renewing of your mind…
Romans 12:1-2 NASB

Our society is focused on self, so much so that we compromise our beliefs and convictions in order to achieve worldly success, which happens to have failure written all over it. As Christians, we should let Him define our success; based on the understanding that true success is only determined by what God is allowed to accomplish in and through us. Who measures your success—the created or the Creator?

66

Because

*But I will not drive them out in a single year, because
the land would become desolate and the wild animals too
numerous for you. Little by little I will drive them
out before you, until you have increased enough
to take possession of the land.*
Exodus 23:29-30 NIV

Today my heart focused on one word 'because.' He has reasons for
taking time to make things happen. He has purpose. Sometimes
revealed and other times not, because you couldn't bear it.
Nuggets digest easier than a load. Struggling with God's timing?
I've got the answer... because.

_____

_____

_____

_____

_____

_____

_____

_____

_____

_____

_____

_____

_____

_____

_____

_____

_____

_____

67

Shadow

He who dwells in the shelter of the Most High will rest
in the shadow of the Almighty.
Psalm 91:1 NIV 1984

The picture that comes to mind from this verse is of a small frail cabin
that looks as though it would offer no resistance to an intruder...
except that looming over it several stories high is a Celestial Warrior
clutching a gleaming sword the size of a tree in one hand and a
fistful of lighting bolts in the other. Ever watchful and fearless is this
Guardian with the single intention of protecting
any who dwells in His shadow.

_____

_____

_____

_____

_____

_____

_____

_____

_____

_____

_____

_____

_____

_____

_____

68

Priorities

Then, leaving her water jar, the woman went back to town and said to the people, "Come, see a man who told me everything I ever did. Could this be the Christ?"
John 4:28-29 NIV 1984

When the Samaritan woman went to the well that day with her water jar, her main priority was to do just that – draw water and return home. Not only did she meet Jesus there, but she learned of the living water that only He can offer. Leaving her water jar behind, she returned to her town to tell her people what she had experienced. Her priorities changed and her life was never the same again. Because of her testimony many came to know Christ. Today give God top priority in your life and you will be changed forever.

_____

_____

_____

_____

_____

_____

_____

_____

_____

_____

_____

_____

_____

_____

_____

Justified

Clearly no one is justified before God by the law,
because, "The righteous will live by faith."
Galatians 3:11 NIV 1984

Be encouraged! You have been justified by His grace in faith alone!
Rest in the Lord for He has justified you and you are an heir having
hope of eternal life! Therefore live today as
an heir of the Most High God.

_____

_____

_____

_____

_____

_____

_____

_____

_____

_____

_____

_____

_____

_____

_____

_____

_____

_____

Today

But seek first His kingdom and His righteousness, and all these things will be given to you as well. Therefore do not worry about tomorrow, for tomorrow will worry about itself. Each day has enough trouble of its own.
Matthew 6:33-34 NIV

So many things can keep us from doing what we are supposed to do today. Worrying about tomorrow and the many overwhelming tasks it brings, paralyzes us from accomplishing the tasks unique to today. Procrastinating, confusing our priorities, and allowing unimportant intrusions all prevent us from living intentionally, for this moment.

Today, let's seek His kingdom and His righteousness first.

71

Defend

*But in your hearts honor Christ the Lord as holy,
always being prepared to make a defense to anyone who
asks you for a reason for the hope that is in you.*
1 Peter 3:15 ESV

If the opportunity to evangelize has not appeared in your life, it will.
People notice that we are different, not of the world. The difficult
task of defending our faith not only challenges the beliefs of others,
but allows us to dig deeper into our own relationship with God,
strengthening the ties that connect us to our Father.

72

Forgiven

And that is what some of you were. But you were washed, you were sanctified, you were justified in the name of the Lord Jesus Christ and by the Spirit of our God.
1 Corinthians 6:11 NIV

It is very comforting to know that no matter how far we have strayed from God, He is faithful to forgive our sins and to forget them. We can't outrun His love no matter how many times we find ourselves fleeing His side. He picks us up and not only dusts us off, but completely cleanses us every single time we fall.

_____

_____

_____

_____

_____

_____

_____

_____

_____

_____

_____

_____

_____

_____

_____

_____

_____

_____

Covered

No temptation has seized you except what is common to man. And God is faithful; He will not let you be tempted beyond what you can bear. But when you are tempted, He will also provide a way out so that you can stand up under it.
1 Corinthians 10:13 NIV 1984

Are you tempted to fear? To give up? To curse God? Don't fret, these temptations are common to man and God is bigger than all of them! He is faithful and He will provide a way out so you can stand.

74

Treasured

For You created my inmost being;
You knit me together in my mother's womb.
Psalm 139:13 NIV

Satan lies to us every day to convince us that we are worthless.
But he is not direct. Instead he tempts us with selfish sin until we fall
then instantly tells us this half truth, "Life is cheap and so are you!"
This is a half truth because you are a work of art molded from a cheap
mound of clay by the Master of all creation.
You are a one of a kind piece of art.

75

Trust

Now the serpent was more crafty than any of the wild
animals the LORD God had made.
He said to the woman, "Did God really say,
'You must not eat from any tree in the garden'?"
Genesis 3:1 NIV

Satan is a one-trick pony. His only ploy is to get you to doubt God.
Every sin can be directly traced back to doubting God's Word.
Trusting His Word when the enemy calls it into question will lead you
to be faithful. Without faith, it is impossible to please God.
Faith is believing His perfect Word.

76

Hands

Can a mother forget the baby at her breast and have no compassion on the child she has borne? Though she may forget, I will not forget you! See, I have engraved you on the palms of My hands; your walls are ever before Me.
Isaiah 49:15-16 NIV

Do you sometimes feel forgotten? Does the work you do seem to go unnoticed? You are not just another face to God. You are significant to Him. He cannot forget you. Your name is engraved on the palms of God's hands. He calls you by name and you are His.

Fear

*Fear not, for I **am** with you; be not dismayed,
for I **am** your God. I will strengthen you, yes,
I will help you,
I will uphold you with My righteous right hand.
Isaiah 41:10 NKJV*

God promises to be with us through every season of life. He promises to strengthen, help and uphold us. God is able to take your fears into His Hand, crush them and blow the dust into thin air. Don't be afraid, He is with you and He knows every detail of what you are going through today.

Foundational

As for God, His way is perfect;
the word of the LORD is flawless.
He is a shield for all who take refuge in Him.
2 Samuel 22:31 NIV 1984

Read carefully what God is offering you; perfection in His way and flawlessness of His word. Who else dares even make an offer like that much less is able to deliver on it? No self-help book, no well-meaning spiritual leader, no man-made set of laws. This is why we must seek God, period. Nothing else gives us a better foundation for life; both present and eternal.

Worthless

Wealth is worthless in the day of wrath,
but righteousness delivers from death.
Proverbs 11:4 NIV

Stuff! Lots and lots of stuff is what we desire, if we are honest.
We are all on that "more" or "new" train that the media tells us we
need to be riding. As soon as you buy something new, in a month it
will be old. When does it end?
Examine your life, your closets, and your garage.
What do you see? What can you clean out?

Sympathize

For we do not have a high priest who is unable to empathize with our weaknesses, but we have One who has been tempted in every way, just as we are—yet He did not sin.
Hebrews 4:15 NIV

It always helps to talk to someone who has been through the valley you are facing. They can give insight, wisdom and encouragement on your darkest days. Jesus has been through the very things that you and I deal with today. Rejection, loneliness, grief, weariness, betrayal, difficult people and sadness were all part of His story. He understands exactly where you are. Pour your heart out to Him. He cares for you.

_____
_____
_____
_____
_____
_____
_____
_____
_____
_____
_____
_____
_____
_____
_____
_____
_____
_____

81

Overwhelmed

*When you pass through the waters, I **will be** with you;*
and through the rivers, they shall not overflow you.
When you walk through the fire, you shall not be burned,
nor shall the flame scorch you.
Isaiah 43:2 NKJV

Life throws some mean punches. It is tempting to look to God and ask, "Why aren't you protecting me?" In that moment, we compare our overwhelming circumstances to how much happier we were before. We must attempt to have perspective and realize all the blessings and safety God has still provided for us, even in our distress. When we thank Him, we feel less overwhelmed.

_____

_____

_____

_____

_____

_____

_____

_____

_____

_____

_____

_____

_____

_____

_____

82

Mercy

He has showed you, O man, what is good. And what does the LORD require of you? To act justly and to love mercy and to walk humbly with your God.
Micah 6:8 NIV 1984

She asked me innocently, "What is mercy?" Following a very difficult journey, which involved helping her mother die a peaceful and pain-free death, we were enjoying a quiet moment, which resulted in that question. I stammered for words. Being the "older" Christian, had I modeled mercy to her? In the constant need-filling role I had played in this journey, had I acted justly and walked humbly with my God? It's all You ask of me, LORD; and yet, it is so very difficult. Help me examine these areas of my life today, LORD. Hold me accountable to honor YOU with every aspect of my life.

83

Steady

He lifted me out of the pit of despair, out of the mud and the mire. He set my feet on solid ground and steadied me as I walked along.
Psalm 40:2 NLT

I was broken; deep in the pit of despair. God didn't pull me out and give me a perfect life. He lifted me out to solid ground and steadied me as I walked. Sometimes I tripped and fell but He always lifted me up again! Is life beating you up? Let Him lift you up and steady your feet. Let Him teach you to walk, one step at a time.

Revealed

But I, the Lord, search all hearts and examine secret motives.
I give all people their due rewards,
according to what their actions deserve.
Jeremiah 17:10 NLT

God is the only One who knows what motivates our thoughts, words, and actions. The Lord examines our motives, so shouldn't we?
We need to act with a right heart (filled with compassion, gentleness, peace, and love) instead of a wrong heart (filled with selfishness, pride, anger, and hate). Our actions have consequences and some of them are eternal. If we ask God, the Spirit will reveal to us what our motives are, right or wrong.

85

Keep Me in Perfect Peace

You will keep him in perfect peace,
Whose mind is stayed on You,
Because he trusts in You.
Isaiah 26:3 NKJV

What occupies your mind and invades your thoughts?
Often times, our minds lead us to worry and that leaves us feeling
discontent and uneasy. Ask God to help you place your thoughts upon
Him and fix your mind on the Lord.
Let the Peacekeeper rule your thoughts and trust in Him.

Transform

Don't copy the behavior and customs of this world,
but let God transform you into a new person by changing the
way you think. Then you will learn to know God's will for
you, which is good and pleasing and perfect.
Romans 12:2 NLT

Be peculiar and contrary. Be off-beat. Different. Listen to the Voice of Truth, not the lies of the world. Trust in the things you can't see, the things that are written on your heart. Let God's Holy Spirit lead you in a new, better way — a way as old as time.

87

Give Thanks!

Give thanks to the LORD for He is good...
Psalm 118:1 NIV

Each day I have the Holy Spirit to guide me into all truth.
God's Word will give me guidance in every situation. God's ear is
attuned to my prayers. God provides the weapons of my warfare to
keep me safe from harm and injury.
God goes before me and comes behind me. He gives me words I
need to speak, the moment I need them. Christ is my Holy Advocate,
standing at the right hand of the Father making intercession for me.
God is due our thanks!

88

Seek

The lions may grow weak and hungry,
but those who seek the LORD lack no good thing.
Psalm 34:10 NIV

The standard rule of the world is the most powerful and fierce, represented here by the lions, are the last to go hungry when times get tough. This verse denies that thought process by reminding us it is the LORD that decides for whom He will provide. Those who seek Him are guaranteed His goodness even when the mighty are lacking. So much changes when we seek to know Him better.
Lives are changed forever.

89

Lost and Found

I will instruct you and teach you in the way you should go...
Psalm 32:8 NIV

I was lost. Who knew that one wrong turn would lead me so far from
my intended destination? I pulled over, plugged my home address into
the navigation feature on my phone, and cranked up the volume.
"At the next intersection, turn right," directed the mechanical voice.
Relief flooded through me; I knew that if I paid attention,
I would be home safe and sound in no time.
God intends His Word to do the same for us.

_____

_____

_____

_____

_____

_____

_____

_____

_____

_____

_____

_____

_____

_____

90

Love One Another

A new command I give you: Love one another.
As I have loved you, so you must love one another.
John 13:34 NIV

How can we do this? Look at Christ!
We are all made in God's image…
and with the Lord's help, all things are possible…
even loving the unlovable.

91

Little Sponges

These commandments that I give you today are to be on your hearts. Impress them on your children.
Deuteronomy 6:6-7a NIV

We never know for sure what things our children are picking up from us. We need to be intentional about the example and teachings we are giving our children. We need to impress upon them the importance of God and His commandments. We should keep Christ centered in our own homes and lives. Children are like sponges and will absorb what is around them. Therefore, look at what is overflowing that your children are soaking up.

_____

_____

_____

_____

_____

_____

_____

_____

_____

_____

_____

_____

_____

_____

_____

_____

92

Childlike

Truly, I say to you, unless you turn and become like children,
you will never enter the kingdom of heaven.
Matthew 18:3 ESV

There is mystery God has not revealed in His Word to us. We will never have all the answers. He says to come unto Him as a little child. Children are eager to learn, trusting, dependent, and are in awe when they sit at our feet to listen and soak in the nuggets we offer from our experience with life. Let's approach Christ as a child.
Will we take Him at His Word?

_____

_____

_____

_____

_____

_____

_____

_____

_____

_____

_____

_____

_____

_____

_____

_____

_____

93

Safe

Trust in Him at all times, you people;
pour out your hearts to Him, for God is our refuge.
Psalm 62:8 NIV

Have you ever poured out your private pain to a friend
only to find out later that she betrayed your confidence?
Truth is...we're all capable of betraying a loved one's trust.
Aren't you glad our Father is 100% trustworthy?
He's a safe place to hide when life gets ugly.
Pour out your heart to Him today, friend.
He's always ready to listen.

94

Wise Woman

She speaks with wisdom, and faithful instruction
is on her tongue.
Proverbs 31:26 NIV

God, let the blessings of Christ's wisdom touch everyone we encounter today. We pray for Your patience and grace to flow from us, especially within our interactions with precious family and friends. Bring peace and serenity to this fresh beginning.

95

Are You Good Soil?

As he was scattering the seed, some fell along the path, and the birds came and ate it up. Some fell on rocky places, where it did not have much soil. Other seed fell among thorns, which grew up and choked the plants. Still other seed fell on good soil, where it produced a crop—a hundred, sixty or thirty times what was sown.
Matthew 13:4-8 NIV

A seed needs a good environment to produce lasting fruit. You must water your soil with the Word of God, a humble posture and a teachable spirit. Are you good soil?

_____

_____

_____

_____

_____

_____

_____

_____

_____

_____

_____

_____

_____

_____

96

Alabaster Love

A woman in that town who lived a sinful life learned that Jesus was eating at the Pharisee's house, so she came there with an alabaster jar of perfume.
Luke 7:37 NIV

The woman who was forgiven of many sins brought Jesus her most precious gift in return. When we begin to fathom the depths of God's gifts, our natural response will be alabaster jar generosity. How will you pour out your gratitude today? Maybe you will love the outcast, buy a cup of coffee for a stranger, or listen to a child's story with undivided attention. Pour out your love in alabaster jar style!

97

All for the Good

And we know that in all things God
works for the good of those who love Him,
who have been called according to His purpose.
Romans 8:28 NIV

In this life there will be many situations that we don't understand.
Horrible things will happen and we will question why.
Though we don't understand, we can have faith in knowing
that God is still in control and He will work it together for good.
God has a plan for everything.

_____

_____

_____

_____

_____

_____

_____

_____

_____

_____

_____

_____

_____

_____

_____

_____

_____

98

On Purpose... Not By Accident

Therefore, beloved, since you look for these things,
be diligent to be found by Him in peace,
spotless and blameless.
2 Peter 3:14 NASB

Oh to be found resting in His "peace," both "spotless and blameless"?
This sinful flesh always seems to get the best of me.
Yet, one day, one glorious day I'll be found perfect and blameless in
His sight. Until then, I must be willing to love, forgive, show kindness,
be rejected, trade my will for His...
REGARDLESS OF THE COST...

_____
_____
_____
_____
_____
_____
_____
_____
_____
_____
_____
_____
_____
_____
_____
_____
_____

99

Who's on Your Throne?

Let us then approach the throne of grace with confidence,
so that we may receive mercy and find grace to help us
in our time of need.
Hebrews 4:16 NIV 1984

I stuck my poor husband up there again. Some days it's my children,
other days it's parents or friends. It is a tall order to ask of a human.
God is the only One who can truly fill that seat.
Who is sitting on your throne? Today let's turn to
the only One who deserves that placement.

Snared

Fear of man will prove to be a snare,
but whoever trusts in the LORD is kept safe.
Proverbs 29:25 NIV

A snare differs from a trap in that a snare will not necessarily wound its victim but only hold it so it can be captured. The fear of man's disapproval snares us and prevents us from seeking eternal matters. Conversely, trusting in the LORD frees us from all earthly shackles. Trust everything about the LORD and you are kept safe of snares because He is Truth, He is Love, He is Forgiveness and He knows no fear.

Accompanied

"Because he loves me," says the LORD, "I will rescue him;
I will protect him, for he acknowledges My name.
He will call upon Me, and I will answer him; I will be with
him in trouble, I will deliver him and honor him."
Psalm 91:14-15 NIV 1984

Memorize Psalm 91. Write it on your heart. Or type it and tuck it in
your back pocket to have with you. Then you can recite it whenever
you get on a plane or in a car or start out on a journey and know that
God is by your side.

_____

_____

_____

_____

_____

_____

_____

_____

_____

_____

_____

_____

_____

Hunger

Man shall not live by bread alone, but by every word
that proceeds from the mouth of God.
Matthew 4:4 NKJV

I enjoy baking but at the end of a hard day, I sometimes take a shortcut and use a cake mix. I trust the company who made the cake mix to have included all the right ingredients and in the right measure, then all I add is the water, oil and eggs. Do we often allow others to determine the ingredients and proper proportions needed for our Christian life? Are we looking for a shortcut instead of feasting on God's Word to satisfy our hunger?

There is no substitute for a personal relationship with God. His Word is our recipe book for an abundant life.

103

Sanctified

… who have been chosen according to the foreknowledge of God the Father, through the sanctifying work of the Spirit, for obedience to Jesus Christ and sprinkling of His blood: Grace and peace be yours in abundance.
1 Peter 1:2 NIV 1984

Daily we are being sanctified by the Holy Trinity. Yield to the working of the Spirit today and grow in His grace. Remember you have personal access to the Father through Jesus Christ our Lord. So run to the Father and be renewed.

104

Baggage

*Then David left his baggage in the care of the baggage
keeper, and ran to the battle line and
entered in order to greet his brothers.*
1 Samuel 17:22 NASB

We all have baggage. It's not the pretty, matching leopard print baggage either. It is heavy, mismatched, taped together, bulky baggage that weighs us down and is embarrassing to claim until the other passengers have left the area. Our baggage may consist of past sin, guilt, shame, and more. Let's take a lesson from David and leave all of our baggage with our Lord, the baggage keeper. Then let's race, unhindered, to the battle line of this life and encourage our brothers!

105

Whisper

... A hurricane wind ripped through the mountains and shattered the rocks before God, but God wasn't to be found in the wind; after the wind an earthquake, but God wasn't in the earthquake; and after the earthquake a fire, but God wasn't in the fire; and after the fire a gentle and quiet whisper.
1 Kings 19:11-12 MSG

God doesn't always call upon us in a mighty way. He calls us in His way. Only He knows who we specifically are capable of reaching. Our purpose is to serve for His glory, no matter how small the task.

Attitude

So the LORD said to Solomon, "Since this is your attitude and you have not kept My covenant and My decrees, which I commanded you, I will most certainly tear the kingdom away from you and give it to one of your subordinates."
1 Kings 11:11 NIV

God values our attitude in everything. Our attitude towards Him can make or break how we receive the blessings He has in store for us. Have you thanked God lately for the blessings He's showered on you in your kingdom?

107

Enlightened

For I will give you words and wisdom that none of your
adversaries will be able to resist or contradict.
Luke 21:15 NIV

The Bible tells us that we will face trials and difficulties in this life and
that we will come across scoffers and unbelievers. But the Bible also
promises that the Holy Spirit will give us the words and wisdom that
we will need in order to be witnesses to them. Whew.
Talk about taking the pressure off. Thank You God.
Relax and allow His love to shine through you like a bright light.

108

Blessing

You will be made rich in every way so that you can be generous on every occasion, and through us your generosity will result in thanksgiving to God.
2 Corinthians 9:11 NIV 1984

"Blessing" is often used as a noun. "That child is a blessing for her."
It's up to us to make it a verb. Don't be a bucket that collects blessings,
but be a pipe through which blessings flow.
God blesses us SO THAT we can pass it on for His glory.
Make your blessings verbs instead of nouns.

109

Inconceivable

However, as it is written: "No eye has seen,
no ear has heard, no mind has conceived
what God has prepared for those who love Him."
1 Corinthians 2:9 NIV 1984

This verse proves beyond any doubt God loves to give good things to His children. As incredible as it seems, the mind, which He created, is not able to even imagine what awaits those who love Him. But wait, there's more! Add to that there will be all of eternity to enjoy it. All this promised by the One who is the personification of faithfulness.

_____

_____

_____

_____

_____

_____

_____

_____

_____

_____

_____

_____

_____

_____

_____

Peace

Peace I leave with you; My peace I give you.
I do not give to you as the world gives.
Do not let your hearts be troubled and do not be afraid.
John 14:27 NIV

The key to peace is not the absence of conflict but the presence of God in our lives through our conflicts. Choosing to turn to God with your troubles instead of focusing on them will keep your heart from being troubled. You do not need to be afraid when you have the Prince of Peace on your side.

Little Sparrow

*Look at the birds. They don't plant or harvest or store food
in barns, for your heavenly Father feeds them.
And aren't you far more valuable to Him than they are?
Matthew 6:26 NLT*

Worry can rob us of our time, energy and joy. Our Father knows what
we need before we even ask. This should remind us that He carefully
watches over us. God holds the future and He knows what is best.
He cares for little birds and His eye is on you too.
Rest in His tender and watchful care today.

_____

_____

_____

_____

_____

_____

_____

_____

_____

_____

_____

_____

_____

_____

_____

_____

Discipline

Whoever loves discipline loves knowledge,
but whoever hates correction is stupid.
Proverbs 12:1 NIV

I read over this and laughed so hard. I had no idea that the word "stupid" was even in the Bible. Do you love discipline? Have you found yourself in that situation where you don't want to be corrected? I think we all have been there. Test the system. The next time someone corrects you, take it in stride, smile and LOVE it.

_____

_____

_____

_____

_____

_____

_____

_____

_____

_____

_____

_____

_____

_____

_____

_____

_____

113

Victory

LORD my God, I called to You for help, and You healed me. You, LORD, brought me up from the realm of the dead; You spared me from going down to the pit.
Psalm 30:2-3 NIV

Victory begins with a cry for help. At the moment we surrender, God begins His work in us. He specializes in resurrecting those parts of our hearts and lives that we thought were dead. Write your prayer of surrender below and give Jesus your broken places.

_____

_____

_____

_____

_____

_____

_____

_____

_____

_____

_____

_____

_____

_____

_____

_____

_____

114

Unblock

For I am persuaded that neither death nor life, nor angels nor
principalities nor powers, nor things present nor things
to come, nor height nor depth, nor any other created thing,
shall be able to separate us from the love of God
which is in Christ Jesus our Lord.
Romans 8:38-39 NKJV

Nothing is blocking us from God's love. That is powerful! At the
core, this means that only we can block ourselves from His love,
by choosing not to accept it. We have a power that nothing else in
creation has. The question is: Why in the world would we reject it?
Whatever misrepresentation of God may have us jaded or confused,
His love is pure, abundant, enduring and guaranteed—
unblock yourself and accept!

What?

The LORD is with me; I will not be afraid.
What can man do to me?
Psalm 118:6 NIV 1984

There is incredible faith found in this verse. The author has
internalized the fact that life for everyone will eventually end and by
his faith in God, his eternal destination is already set. Having those
two foundational truths settled leaves nothing else to fear because God
is in control. This person is steady, not shaken by life, not tossed by the
wind, just confident in God's abilities. Like the deep-rooted tree on
the riverbank: none of its leaves wither.

_____

_____

_____

_____

_____

_____

_____

_____

_____

_____

_____

_____

_____

_____

_____

_____

_____

Rel^ationship ~~igion~~

But God is so rich in mercy… even though we were dead because of our sins, He gave us life when He raised Christ from the dead…
Ephesians 2:4-5 NLT

I was dead; entangled in the sin of sexual promiscuity, hoping it would bring me true love. Instead I found emptiness and shame. Then I met Jesus who showed me love by dying on a cross for the very sin that entangled me. I didn't find a religion; I found true love.
I found a relationship beyond my wildest dreams.
Will you let Him love you like no one else can?

_____

_____

_____

_____

_____

_____

_____

_____

_____

_____

_____

_____

_____

_____

_____

_____

_____

Forgiven

If we confess our sins, He is faithful and just and will forgive us our sins and purify us from all unrighteousness.
1 John 1:9 NIV

Do you ever feel beside yourself with sadness because you know you just blew it and were not Christ-like at all? It's ok. God knows that we are not perfect and that we will make mistakes. He is bigger than our mistakes, and He loves you so much. Simply go to Him, confess your sins and rest in His forgiveness. He is faithful and good all the time.

118

Forgiven and Debt Free

Then Peter came to him and asked, "Lord, how often should I forgive someone who sins against me? Seven times?"
"No, not seven times," Jesus replied,
"but seventy times seven!"
Matthew 18:21-22 NLT

Jesus says we are to forgive 7 x 70 times which is equivalent to "always." If we don't forgive, we'll eventually be filled with anger and bitterness. To forgive is the decision to cancel a debt, a debt that is impossible to repay anyway. How do you quantify the pain someone has caused you? How do you convert your pain into retribution? Jesus cancelled our debt, so shouldn't we?

_____

_____

_____

_____

_____

_____

_____

_____

_____

_____

_____

_____

_____

_____

_____

_____

The One Who Goes Before You

And the LORD, He is the One who goes before you.
He will be with you. He will not leave you nor forsake you;
do not fear nor be dismayed.
Deuteronomy 31:8 NKJV

In an ever-changing and static world, isn't it good to know that the
Lord is the One who has gone before you? You have no need to
worry or fear, because He has promised to never leave or forsake
you. Ask Him to surround you with His peace and presence and
know that whatever you face today, He has already gone before you.

Rest

*Come to Me, all you who are weary and burdened, and I
will give you rest. Take My yoke upon you and learn from
Me, for I am gentle and humble in heart,
and you will find rest for your souls.*
Matthew 11:28-29 NIV

Jesus knows the feeling of a lump in the throat, of stinging eyes and a
grieving heart. If your shoulders ache from the weight, He will carry
your buckets of disappointment, or loneliness, or shame. He will teach
you how to set them down, and show you how to walk in a new way.

121

Words

Let your speech be always with grace...
Colossians 4:6 KJV

We've all heard the myth that words should not hurt us. But they do. People who are hurting or have blown it time and time again don't need to know what they have done wrong. They need to know they are loved and they are forgiven. That is why our words to others, as Christians, should be gracious and seasoned with salt.

Rather than quoting the local news, let us quote God's Word and provide a reason for hope and redemption to our world.

122

All

I sought the LORD, and He answered me;
He delivered me from all my fears.
Psalm 34:4 NIV

Think how much fear can control our lives. There's the fear of failure,
rejection, loneliness, aging and death. Each of them rob us of being all
God enables us to be, unless we have asked to be delivered. Once you
have sought and embraced His unconditional love, no fear can challenge
you that His love cannot conquer. Name your fear;
His love overcomes it. Once God owns you, fear cannot;
no more than darkness may be found in light.

123

Trail Guide

When you pass through the waters, I will be with you;
and through the rivers, they shall not overwhelm you;
when you walk through fire you shall not be burned,
and the flame shall not consume you.
Isaiah 43:2 NRSV

To paraphrase the song, we were never promised a rose garden.
But what we are promised is a trail guide, someone to lead us along
the path, even when we can't see it. God never guaranteed an easy
life (Can I get an Amen?) but His Word says we never take one step
without Him by our side.

_____

_____

_____

_____

_____

_____

_____

_____

_____

_____

_____

_____

_____

_____

_____

124

He Cares

Cast all your anxiety on him because he cares for you.
1 Peter 5:7 NIV

We should never carry our burdens alone.
God hears each and every prayer and He hurts when we hurt.
Step out in faith and know our Lord wants to take the weight off our
shoulders. All we need to do is trust in Him.
What peace that brings!

Get Moving

Tell the Israelites to move on.
Exodus 14:15b NIV

Even as bad as being enslaved was for the Israelites, they wanted to go back. Moses didn't think that they should go back; he felt they should simply stand still and wait. However, the Lord said for them to "move on." It's easy to stand still or go back. However, you will never get to your "promise land" if you don't take that step of faith. God has big things in store for each of us. However, those blessings will not be realized if we never get moving.

Faith

As the body without the spirit is dead,
so faith without deeds is dead.
James 2:26 NIV

You believe that there is one God. Good!
Even the demons believe that—and shudder.
James 2:19 NIV

Faith believes in something that can't be seen. Obedience and desire are kindled when true faith is born. Anyone can claim to be a Christ follower. Even demons believe there is one God and they shudder. Out of the heart comes the overflow of true faith. Attitudes, actions, words, and desires are evidences of faith. Is my confidence in Christ?

_____

_____

_____

_____

_____

_____

_____

_____

_____

_____

_____

_____

_____

_____

127

I Must Confess

Search me, God, and know my heart; test me and know my anxious thoughts. See if there is any offensive way in me, and lead me in the way everlasting.
Psalm 139:23-24 NIV

Does your heart feel heavy and out-of-sorts? Has grumbling replaced your gratitude? Are you having trouble praying? Perhaps it's time to let God do some spring cleaning in your heart. Sometimes, we let unaddressed sin build up until it settles like smog over our souls. Why not fling open the windows and let the Spirit clear the air? Soon, your heart will be back in the joy business.

Radiant

Those who look to Him are radiant;
their faces are never covered with shame.
Psalm 34:5 NIV

Understanding a specific word used in this verse is important.
When light shines upon something, the object is illuminated.
When light shines against something, the light is reflected. When light
fills or inhabits something, then that object or person radiates light.
Their faces are not able to express shame, fear, bitterness, or envy
because the light inside is more powerful than merely emotion.
You will long remember meeting a radiant person just as the earth
remains warm long after the sun sets.

129

Her Hands

Honor her for all that her hands have done,
and let her works bring her praise at the city gate.
Proverbs 31:31 NIV

God wants us to share His love by serving others. As you go through your day, look for opportunities to encourage and bless those around you in Jesus' name. A simple note of encouragement, the delight of lunch bought for the car behind you at the drive-thru, or volunteering within your church provide just a few examples. What gifts, talents or passions has God placed in your heart for a moment such as this?

Abiding in Christ

I am the vine; you are the branches.
If you remain in Me and I in you, you will bear much fruit;
apart from Me you can do nothing.
John 15:5 NIV

To abide means "to wait for; to endure without yielding."
When I remain connected to God, He provides all of my needs in His
timing. When I run ahead of God, I detach myself from Him instead
of waiting for God's direction. I wither and crave His life giving water.
Are you attached to the Vine? Or are you withering from your
detachment from Him?

_____

_____

_____

_____

_____

_____

_____

_____

_____

_____

_____

_____

_____

_____

_____

_____

_____

_____

Honor

Do you not know that your bodies are temples of the Holy Spirit, who is in you, whom you have received from God? You are not your own; you were bought at a price. Therefore honor God with your bodies.
1 Corinthians 6:19-20 NIV

Have you ever driven a jalopy? You sweat as you turn the key. You breathe when you hear the engine respond. Why? You have places to go. You are needed! Similarly, your body is a vehicle for God's Spirit to touch this world in ways only you can.
Honor God with your body!

132

A New Creation

Therefore, if anyone is in Christ, he is a new creation.
The old has passed away; behold, the new has come.
2 Corinthians 5:17 ESV

When we surrender our lives to the Lord, He will begin to change us.
We will no longer be the same as we were before we came to Him.
He will purify our hearts to make us more like Him.
We will be made new in Him!

133

This Little Light of Mine

When Christ, who is our life, is revealed,
then you also will be revealed with Him in glory.
Colossians 3:4 NASB

Do you feel unappreciated? Or even worse… unseen?
One day, Jesus will reveal Himself and His truth to the world. At that
knowledge every knee will bow. When the world sees Christ for who
He really is… they too will see us for who we really are…
joint-heirs with Christ. What was hidden by darkness will become
radiant in His pure light!
Why wait? Let's light this world until He is seen.

Do-Over

"Then neither do I condemn you," Jesus declared.
"Go now and leave your life of sin."
John 8:11b NIV

The adulterous woman didn't want to be caught red-handed or put
on display, yet God used that circumstance to set her free.
It was her time. Would you like a do-over? Life can get so tangled
that you wonder if it can ever be straightened out. Take heart!
The Bible is slam packed with examples of do-overs and second
chances. Today He's ready to set you free. It's your time.

135

Upheld

If the Lord delights in a man's way, He makes his steps firm;
though he stumble, he will not fall,
for the LORD upholds him with His hand.
Psalm 37:23-24 NIV 1984

It is critical to our spiritual walk that we understand Scripture does not promise smooth seas and cloudless days; what is promised is support. To uphold someone is to prevent them from sinking or falling. God's intent is for us to grow and growing includes unsteadiness. In His infinite goodness, God knows when to extend His hand. Let that knowledge be the foundation of your assurance.

_____

_____

_____

_____

_____

_____

_____

_____

_____

_____

_____

_____

_____

_____

136

Got Armor?

Put on the full armor of God so that you can
take your stand against the devil's schemes.
Ephesians 6:11 NIV

God furnishes our armor without a trip to the store to buy it. He has thought of everything we need to get through our day and keep Satan's darts from penetrating our hearts. Before you get out of bed in the morning, visually put on each piece of armor in prayer. You will need the breastplate of righteousness, the helmet of salvation, the sword of the Spirit, the shield of faith, the shoes of peace, the belt of truth, and prayer. You don't want to be on the battlefield without a way to communicate with the Commander (God). Prayer is your lifeline. God equips us to win the battle. Take time daily to suit up!

137

Glorified

I consider that our present sufferings are not worth comparing with the glory that will be revealed in us.
Romans 8:18 NIV

In today's failing economy and job losses, remember that in Christ you have an inheritance that can never perish, spoil or fade - kept in heaven for you. One day, in Him, you will be completely glorified. Keep your eyes on Him as He moves you from glory to glory.

Accompanied

Where can I go from Your Spirit?
Where can I flee from Your presence?
Psalm 139:7 NIV

Once you ask Jesus Christ into your heart and accept Him as your Lord and Savior, He will send the Holy Spirit to be your Comforter and Counselor. Then there is literally nowhere which you can go and be away from His Spirit. You may not always feel that He is there but His Word promises that He is with you always. So rest in peace and know that you will never again be alone.

Peace

*Grace to you and peace from God our Father and
the Lord Jesus Christ.
Ephesians 1:2 NASB*

A lone duck glides along the middle of the calm lake, a rose bush is
bursting with glorious yellow blooms, the sun is out after two days
of rain, and the morning is still and quiet. Ten little ducklings toddle
furiously along the shoreline trying to keep up with their momma,
spring flowers have budded, and the air is moist and fragrant.
It is spring, and I am blessed to observe it. Winter has passed and once
again, the Father has approved the arrival of
a season of life and grace and peace.

140

Yet

*"Though the mountains be shaken and the hills be removed,
yet My unfailing love for you will not be shaken nor My
covenant of peace be removed," says the LORD,
who has compassion on you.*
Isaiah 54:10 NIV

Anyone having seen before-and-after pictures of Mount St. Helens
knows the effect of a "hill being removed" yet, regardless of the most
cataclysmic life-changing upheavals you can imagine, God's love
for you goes unchanged. No hairline cracks in His forgiveness or
qualifiers in His promises to you.
You will never experience love more unfailing than His.

_____

_____

_____

_____

_____

_____

_____

_____

_____

_____

_____

_____

_____

_____

_____

_____

141

Journey

*When you pass through the waters, I **will be** with you;*
And through the rivers, they shall not overflow you.
When you walk through the fire, you shall not be burned,
Nor shall the flame scorch you.
Isaiah 43:2 NKJV

God fights for us. He protects us from our enemies and accompanies us on all our journeys. Not only will He be with us daily, but throughout eternity. We are safe and guarded in Him, by Him.

_____

_____

_____

_____

_____

_____

_____

_____

_____

_____

_____

_____

_____

_____

_____

_____

Holy

May He strengthen your hearts so that you will be blameless and holy in the presence of our God and Father when our Lord Jesus comes with all His holy ones.
1 Thessalonians 3:13 NIV

I don't know about you, but I am eternally grateful that Jesus Christ is my Lord and Savior. I am holy and blameless. What an amazing day it will be to physically hear God's voice with my ears say that my sins are forgiven. Hallelujah!

143

Gifted

He replied, "I tell you that to everyone who has,
more will be given, but as for the one who has nothing,
even what he has will be taken away."
Luke 19:26 NIV 1984

God has gifted you with talents and abilities which can be used to grow His kingdom. If you do what comes easy and natural, and you purposefully do it for His glory, then you will find yourself doing things you never dreamed you could do. Be faithful in what He has gifted you to do and He will multiply your talents in an amazing way.

144

Assured

"For My thoughts are not your thoughts,
neither are your ways My ways," declares the LORD.
Isaiah 55:8 NIV

Think of the last time in your life when the way forward was unclear
or uncertain. These times are used by God to refine us.

Our will naturally seeks to be in control, yet we struggle with the
insecurity that comes when we are in control. God is infinitely aware
of our lives and His knowledge of us is perfect! That means He knows
exactly what we need now, based on our past, to assure our future.

_____

_____

_____

_____

_____

_____

_____

_____

_____

_____

_____

_____

_____

_____

_____

_____

_____

_____

_____

145

Stand

Finally, be strong in the Lord and in His mighty power.
Put on the full armor of God so that you can take your stand
against the devil's schemes.
Ephesians 6:10-11 NIV

You and I are in a battle with unseen forces. The devil tells you,
"It's a losing battle so why fight?" The Lord says, "Be strong and put
your trust in My mighty power." Someone once said, "If you don't
stand for something you will fall for anything."
Use the armor He has given you and take your stand.

Refuge

The LORD is a refuge for the oppressed,
a stronghold in times of trouble.
Psalm 9:9 NIV

To best grasp the beauty of this verse, we should focus on the
definition of a refuge. It is more than a temporary shelter. It is more
than simply stacking furniture against the door as trouble continues to
batter its way in. A refuge is a safe place; a place for healing;
a soothing source of comfort. The refuge exists because the
Stronghold surrounds it; a Stronghold impervious to attack. The
enemy views this Stronghold and abandons its efforts. You are safe!

147

Perfect?

As parents feel for their children,
God feels for those who fear Him.
He knows us inside and out,
keeps in mind that we're made of mud.
Psalm 103:13-14 MSG

Do you ever become discouraged at your faults, mistakes and sins?
Me too. But God reminds us that He loves us with deep compassion.
He knows how He made us. He knows everything about us, even
how many hairs are on our heads. He loves us in spite of our
imperfections. Turn your focus back on Him
knowing that He accepts you, you're His and He loves you!

Dependable

The grass withers and the flowers fall,
but the Word of God stands forever.
Isaiah 40:8 NIV 1984

Nothing is as flawless and dependable as the Word of God. It guides
you, it instructs you, it rebukes, it trains you. It encourages you,
it comforts you and lifts you up. It gives you hope and joy and peace
and love. You can find all these things as well as your awesome Father
in the pages of the Bible. What are you waiting for?
Get yours, open it up and discover what awaits you today.

149

Peace

A heart at peace gives life to the body,
but envy rots the bones.
Proverbs 14:30 NIV

Ever wish to be in someone else's shoes? The grass always seems to be
less prickly in someone else's yard. Peace is difficult to grasp.
Look at your life, and acknowledge the fact that no one else has been
on your journey. God wouldn't want it any other way.
He can use you just as you are and because of the past you have.
Receive the peace He wants to give to you today.

_____

_____

_____

_____

_____

_____

_____

_____

_____

_____

_____

_____

_____

_____

_____

_____

150

Anger

We always carry around in our body the death of Jesus,
so that the life of Jesus may also be revealed in our body.
2 Corinthians 4:10 NIV

You can tell a lot about a person by watching how they act.
If you are harboring anger or resentment, eventually you will yell
at your kids or be short with your spouse. What is in our hearts will
eventually spill out. So, how would life look differently if we carried
around the sacrifice of Jesus in our hearts? If we let His atoning
sacrifice govern our actions, our thoughts and our attitudes? Maybe
it's time to repent for letting our emotions rule and truly ask Jesus to
take control of our lives and be on display through us.
What are you carrying around with you?

151

Flow

Be anxious for nothing, but in everything by prayer
and supplication, with thanksgiving,
let your requests be known to God; and the peace of God,
which surpasses all understanding,
will guard your hearts and minds through Christ Jesus.
Philippians 4:6-7 NKJV

Don't hold back. He is the one phone line that is always open.
He always understands and He always responds with the right answer
(imagine that): "I love you." There isn't anything He cannot handle—
let it flow. The peace that comes from a simple, sincere,
irrevocable "I love you," is the peace you desire.

152

Heights

The Sovereign LORD is my strength; He makes my feet like the feet of a deer, He enables me to go on the heights.
Habakkuk 3:19 NIV 1984

The feet of a mountain dwelling deer are certainly unique in their creation. Their design gives them the ability to go places that defy belief. At times it can spare their lives from an enemy. God's strength grants us the same amazing spiritual capabilities. Challenges that once would have immobilized us with fear no longer tower over us. In awe, we find ourselves scaling the heights.

153

Exalted

Humble yourselves, therefore, under God's mighty hand,
that He may lift you up in due time.
1 Peter 5:6 NIV

Being humbled is seldom an enjoyable experience. It can, and usually does, bring you to your knees. But take heart. God has a reason for humbling you. He humbles you so that He can later exalt you but still receive all the glory. If you are a believer in Jesus Christ you can count on being humbled, but you can also count on being given a wealth of blessings in God's due time.

154

Renewed

Put on your new nature, and be renewed
as you learn to know your Creator and become like Him.
Colossians 3:10 NLT

Reading the Word of God and studying Scripture is not something
we do just for the sake of doing. It is for being renewed!
The dictionary defines renewed as to begin again or become new.
Do you feel like you need a fresh start? A do over? Spending time in
the Word allows us to learn to know our Creator and thus become
new... become like Him.

Doorkeeper

Better is one day in Your courts than a thousand elsewhere;
I would rather be a doorkeeper in the house of my God than
dwell in the tents of the wicked.
Psalm 84:10 NIV

What a contrast to today's thinking. The author would sooner have
the most menial position in the temple than a recognized position of
status associating with the deceiving crowd. Why? Because God loves
with no strings attached; no one gets preferential treatment.
The doorkeeper receives no less grace than the king. All who worship
Him feast at the Lord's banquet table and experience His paradise.

Good Courage

Wait patiently for the Lord. Be brave and courageous.
Yes, wait patiently for the LORD.
Psalm 27:14 NLT

Waiting on the Lord does not come naturally. After receiving Christ, it is no longer about what we want, but what He wants for us. Are you still waiting on what you want? Be strengthened by His kindness as He gives you the things He wants you to have. To be of good courage refers to a Spirit-produced inner confidence.
If we stay in Him and His Word, we can ask whatever we wish and it will be done for us (John 15:7).

157

Quiet Me with Your Love

The LORD your God in your midst,
The Mighty One, will save;
He will rejoice over you with gladness,
He will quiet you with His love,
He will rejoice over you with singing.
Zephaniah 3:17 NKJV

When you feel troubled and this world gets too noisy,
run to the Lord and find solitude in Him. Let Him quiet your soul
with His love and know that He is in your midst. Listen as He rejoices
over you with gladness and be refreshed as the outside noise fades
away in His presence.

Secure

My Father, Who has given them to Me, is greater than all;
no one can snatch them out of My Father's hand.
John 10:29 NIV

Yes, you will have many troubles in this world. You will be tempted
to sin, you will sin. But take heart. Once you belong to the Father, no
one and nothing can snatch you from His hand.
He is always with you, guiding you and protecting you,
giving you wisdom and guidance. So be BOLD in your faith and
keep your eyes on our Great God.

159

Small

"For My thoughts are not your thoughts, neither are your ways My ways," declares the LORD. "As the heavens are higher than the earth, so are My ways higher than your ways and My thoughts higher than your thoughts."
Isaiah 55:8-9 NIV

Sometimes there is a comfort in being small. You are not expected to carry as much, if you are small. And you don't have to have all the answers. And you can find rest, in the shadow of another, if you are small. We must feel our own smallness, to know of His greatness.

160

Second Chances

*But go your way; tell His disciples and
Peter that He goeth before you…*
Mark 16:7 KJV

Peter had denied Jesus, not once or twice but three times. Could that betrayal be forgiven? What would Peter have to do to be back in the graces of our Lord? Just like you and me, Peter was forgiven due to his contrite heart and his confession. Later in Scripture, Jesus asked Peter three times if he loved Him. Three times denied… three times love confessed. God is the God of second chances. Just ask Jonah, Moses, Joseph, Peter… and me.

Perfection

To all perfection I see a limit;
but Your commands are boundless.
Psalm 119:96 NIV 1984

One limit of human perfection is it can never be achieved. If there is a lesson perfection can teach, it is that the pursuit of it is meaningless: a chasing after the wind. God's commands, on the other hand, are boundless in their lessons. Each precept we obey yields a wealth of knowledge about living with each other and how to restrain our selfish nature. By accepting God's grace, we gain release from the chains of perfection to flourish in the lushness of His commands.

162

Burn Out

If anyone serves, they should do so with the strength God provides, so that in all things God may be praised through Jesus Christ.
1 Peter 4:11b NIV

Ever get so busy for Jesus you don't have time for Him? Okay, maybe that's just me. Serving, even in church, won't always feel like a party. But when the joy is gone and we are exhausted, it's time to step back and reevaluate. Serve with the strength He provides, for His glory, not in your strength for your glory. He doesn't need us to make Him look good.

163

Sustained

Cast your cares on the LORD and He will sustain you;
He will never let the righteous fall.
Psalm 55:22 NIV 1984

Do you trust in the Lord alone? If so, He will never let you fall.
You are righteous because Jesus, the Lamb is righteous.
Lay your burdens down before the LORD, and ask for His wisdom and
guidance, and then rest, waiting for the discernment
which He will provide. He cares for you, like none other.

Stop the Comparison Game

*Then they should take pride in themselves alone,
without comparing themselves to someone else.*
Galatians 6:4b NIV

So often the comparison game is played by looking at someone on the outside – appearance, job, possessions and talents. We need to keep in mind that God created and gifted each of us specifically for His unique purpose and plan. Do not spend your time second guessing God's design. He doesn't make mistakes. Christ's example will push you to do your best and His grace and unending love for you will bring comfort when you fall short of your expectations.

_____
_____
_____
_____
_____
_____
_____
_____
_____
_____
_____
_____
_____
_____
_____
_____
_____
_____

165

Words

*But the wisdom that comes from heaven is first of all pure;
then peace-loving, considerate, submissive, full of mercy and
good fruit, impartial and sincere.*
James 3:17 NIV

Spoken words have power to light a harmful, consuming fire, or to
snuff out a spark. Words spoken in anger or frustration cannot be
retrieved. Let the Holy Spirit bring words that are pure, peace-loving,
considerate, submissive, full of mercy, good, impartial, and sincere.
Teach us, Lord, to draw from Your heart each time we speak.
Teach us to measure our words carefully.

166

Blanketed

But let all who take refuge in You be glad; let them ever sing for joy. Spread Your protection over them, that those who love Your name may rejoice in You.
Psalm 5:11 NIV

Is there any more secure feeling than being covered with a blanket? Whether cold, feeling ill, or simply exhausted at the end of the day, the world's problems shrink when we are wrapped tightly. That is the image portrayed here, only the One tucking you in is God Himself using a spread of the strongest armor yet quilted with assurance and lined with love.

_____

_____

_____

_____

_____

_____

_____

_____

_____

_____

_____

_____

_____

_____

_____

_____

_____

Young at Heart

Therefore we do not lose heart.
Though outwardly we are wasting away,
yet inwardly we are being renewed day by day.
2 Corinthians 4:16 NIV

ach morning, my creaky joints remind me I'm getting older.
But, somehow, my heart feels younger and feistier with every birthday.
How can that be? It's Jesus. The more I get to know Him, the more
I'm changed inside. I may not move as quickly as I used to,
but my heart leaps like a frisky lamb.
What hope we have as daughters of God!

168

Go Bananas

Be joyful in hope, patient in affliction, faithful in prayer.
Romans 12:12 NIV

As a girl making my first dessert, I learned a lesson about following instructions and key ingredients. My completed banana pie looked beautiful and delicious. But it was not the pie it could have been, all because of a missing ingredient. Can you guess? Yep. Bananas.

Romans 12:12 reminds us to invite not one, but all of these ingredients into our lives. Sweet friend, imagine the extraordinary

_____

_____

_____

_____

_____

_____

_____

_____

_____

_____

_____

_____

_____

_____

_____

_____

_____

_____

169

Healed

Reckless words pierce like a sword, but
the tongue of the wise brings healing.
Proverbs 12:18 NIV 1984

When we are hurt by others' words or actions our natural defense is to
retaliate, often with hurtful words. Even though this may "feel good"
at the time, nothing good will come of it, in fact it only serves to make
matters worse. Instead, when you are hurt by someone's words, run to
Jesus and tell Him. And allow Him to apply His ointment which will
bring about true healing. The quicker you go to the Great Physician,
the quicker the healing.

170

Powerful Words

Don't use foul or abusive language.
Let everything you say be good and helpful, so that
your words will be an encouragement to those who hear them.
Ephesians 4:29 NLT

Sticks and stones may break my bones… and words can hurt even more. Our words are like a surgeon's scalpel. Used the way God intended, they can heal a heart. But if they are in careless hands, they can wound deeply. Consider each person whose path you will cross today. Whether they are family, friends, coworkers, or strangers, use your words to encourage, affirm, and heal.

171

Satisfying

You open Your hand and satisfy the desires
of every living thing.
Psalm 145:16 NIV

It is little wonder that our limited minds have a difficult time grasping
the concept of God's immensity. This verse paints a humbling word
picture of just one facet of His amazing abilities. At the simple act of
opening His hand every living thing finds satisfaction. Not only those
beings the world deems to be important, beautiful, or talented but all
that lives. There is no discrimination, God is all inclusive.
Mysteriously, He can satisfy desires we are not even aware we have
until we know Him.

God's Lavishing Love

See what great love the Father has lavished on us,
that we should be called children of God!
And that is what we are!
1 John 3:1 NIV

Children know their fathers love them by their actions. Fathers don't just say they love their children, but they demonstrate it through loving actions. In the same way, God demonstrated His love for us through His Son's death on the cross. We show our love for God through our actions towards others. Have you received the Father's love? In what ways do you express your love for God?

173

Guided

Jesus answered, "I am the way and the truth and the life.
No one comes to the Father except through me."
John 14:6 NIV

Focus your thoughts on Jesus each day, allowing Him to accompany
you on your journey. He is the Way and the Truth and the Life.
Enjoy the knowledge that He is in control and that He loves you and
cares for you and will protect and guide you.
Delight yourself in the Lord and your joy will abound.

174

Surrounded

*The angel of the LORD encamps around those
who fear Him, and He delivers them.
Psalm 34:7 NIV*

We have all heard of the preparation that takes place preceding a presidential visit. No detail is overlooked, every precaution is taken. In the verse above, you are the dignitary and God Himself provides for the security coverage. Not only are you delivered, you are not even aware of thwarted ambushes or harmful threats made upon you. His angel handles it: around the clock, all year long. There exists no better protection than that the LORD bestows on His children.

175

Tomorrow

Therefore do not worry about tomorrow,
for tomorrow will worry about itself.
Each day has enough trouble of its own.
Matthew 6:34 NIV

We spend entirely too much time worrying about things that may or
may not happen in the future. Scripture clearly tells us not to worry
about tomorrow because each day has enough trouble of its own.
We need to take our focus off of what may come about in the future
and focus on what is happening right now, today. If tomorrow never
comes, we wasted today worrying for no reason.

Free

God made Him who had no sin to be sin for us,
so that in Him we might become the righteousness of God.
2 Corinthians 5:21 NIV

He took our sin and gave us His righteousness in return. When we wallow in guilt over our sin it is as if we are saying "no thank you" to this amazing gift. Jesus doesn't want you to wallow in your brokenness, feeling unworthy and worthless. He wants you to be FREE! Free to look to Him, trust in Him and live an abundant life full of Joy and Peace and Love.

177

Shepherds

Then I will give you shepherds after My own heart,
who will lead you with knowledge and understanding.
Jeremiah 3:15 NIV

It is interesting to see what God does not say He will give us.
It does not say shepherds who are talented speakers, will make us feel
good, or perform great signs and wonders. God knows all those things
fade. He would rather we trust in knowledge and understanding.
When the storm is fierce we can know our foundation is
superior and our outcome assured. That understanding is the root
of our joy and peace.

Get Rid of it!

*... but everyone, after he has been fully trained,
will be like his teacher.*
Luke 6:40 NASB

Why has society strayed from the foundation on which it was built?
At conception, we are all fully trained sinners – master students of
Satan's teachings. Seems hopeless right?

Ephesians 4:20-24 MSG

*... everything—and I do mean everything—connected with
that old way of life has to go... then take on... a God-
fashioned life, a life renewed from the inside and working
itself into your conduct as God accurately reproduces His
character in you.*

179

I Am a Willow

Let us acknowledge the LORD; let us press on to
acknowledge Him. As surely as the sun rises,
He will appear; He will come to us like the winter rains,
like the spring rains that water the earth.
Hosea 6:3 NIV

I am a willow. Over the years the wind has blown ferociously causing me to bend and sway. Occasionally a major trial has left me broken but not defeated. Life happens, the winds blow and rain comes crashing down and yet we continue to reach ever upward, pressing on.

Taste

Taste and see that the LORD is good;
blessed is the man who takes refuge in Him.
Psalm 34:8 NIV 1984

God is fully open to anyone who has doubts or simply questions about how faith fits life. The author suggests we taste and know for ourselves His goodness. Something can look, feel, and smell good but the final determination is to taste it. God is confident in this challenge because He created us and understands what we crave – unconditional love. Neither is He afraid of us tasting anything else and finding something more satisfying than Him.

That will never happen.

Keys

I will give you the keys of the kingdom of heaven…
Matthew 16:19 NIV

I remember well my first job at sixteen years old. One day my boss handed me the keys to our office building and with those keys came both a privilege and a responsibility. When Peter confessed, "You are the Christ," Jesus replied, "I will give you the keys to the kingdom of heaven." As His disciples, we too, have had keys placed in our hands. What a privilege and responsibility as we sit at His table and become heirs of His kingdom. How do you take care of these keys that have been handed to you? Let us strive to open the door for others so that they may receive their set of keys.

182

Freedom

It is for freedom that Christ has set us free.
Stand firm, then, and do not let yourselves
be burdened again by a yoke of slavery.
Galatians 5:1 NIV

The enemy of this world wants nothing more than to keep you in the
bondage of sin. Stand firm, Christ Jesus has set you free!
Go and sin no more!

183

Redeemed

Therefore, there is now no condemnation
for those who are in Christ Jesus.
Romans 8:1 NIV

We have all sinned and yet we find it easy to condemn others for
their sins. If you have sinned, try not to worry or listen to the
condemnation of others. Instead, immediately take it to the throne
of grace and confess it before the Lord. Then turn from your sin
and walk away, because there is no condemnation in Christ Jesus.
Through Christ Jesus, we are set free from the law of sin and death.

184

Sanctuary

Thus I have seen You in the sanctuary,
To see Your power and Your glory.
Psalm 63:2 NASB

One afternoon we were watching a spring thunderstorm rolling toward us. These are truly a majestic and powerful beauty to behold in our part of the world. Plenty of sky and few trees make for a massive, unhindered canvas. Expansive brush strokes of monstrous dark blue and green clouds swept away the lighter blue sky as the storm built and made its way across the dusty landscape.

Here and there, bright yellow, narrow rays of sunshine flashed forcefully through the imposing cloud ceiling, and I thanked God for allowing me a glimpse into His magnificent sanctuary.

185

Rescue

Even to your old age and gray hairs I am He, I am He who will sustain you. I have made you and I will carry you; I will sustain you and I will rescue you.
Isaiah 46:4 NIV

Another benefit to God's promises is there are no time limitations, no shelf life, no best-if-used-by date, and no expiration, yet it can frighten us to realize we will require nearly as much help in our old age as when we were newborn. God knows that. Not only is He is okay with it, He looks forward to having us in His arms.

Waiting

Wait on the LORD; Be of good courage,
And He shall strengthen your heart;
Wait, I say, on the LORD!
Psalm 27:14 NKJV

Staying with God's plan can be tiring. I waited on God for six years. Through those grueling years I pursued Him and built a solid foundation in my faith. Looking back and seeing the outcome is easier when the experience has passed. We live in a fast paced world. Waiting on God means letting Him take control of our life and watching Him fulfill our needs in His own time.

187

Positive

*For seven days they celebrated with joy the Feast of
Unleavened Bread, because the LORD had filled them with
joy by changing the attitude of the king of Assyria,
so that he assisted them in the work on the house of God,
the God of Israel.*
Ezra 6:22 NIV 1984

A good outlook is a gauge of God's importance in your life.
When people see a change in behavior, they desire to know the
source. The Lord will fill you with joy by changing the attitudes of
those around you as well.

Omnipresent

Evening, morning and noon, I cry out in distress,
and He hears my voice.
Psalm 55:17 NIV

God is ALWAYS there, in good times and in bad, in quiet times and in the midst of chaos. He is always there and He loves you. He wants you to cry out to Him, to seek His help, and to trust that He is there, protecting you, and providing your every need. You can cry out to Him anytime of the day or night and He will hear your cry. And He will be there, by your side.

189

Strength

I can do all things through Christ who strengthens me.
Philippians 4:13 NKJV

When you are faced with an "I can't" situation, remember that with
Christ you "can" do all things He is calling you to do.
Lean not on your own understanding.
God sees the big picture while we focus on the little dot of color.
Trust Him. Rely on His strength to get you through.

Shine

Thus let all Your enemies perish, O LORD!
*But **let** those who love Him **be** like the sun when it*
comes out in full strength...
Judges 5:31 NKJV

There is nothing more beautiful than the sun returning after a summertime thunderstorm. Its bright rays reach through dark clouds. It shines brightly to chase away the darkness and rain. Don't let your circumstances bring dark clouds to cover your light. Someone needs your smile, your touch, your encouragement today.
Someone needs to see your love for God shine like the sun when it comes out in full strength.

191

Knowing

Do you know when the mountain goats give birth?
Do you watch when the doe bears her fawn?
Do you count the months till they bear?
Do you know the time they give birth?
Job 39:1-2 NIV

This rhetorical questioning of Job by God should catch our attention.
To all of these questions Job can only answer "no" so it stands to
reason that God answers by contrast, "I do." Only a profoundly loving
God counts the months of a doe's pregnancy.
Can you sense how intimate God is with His creation,
of which you have been called His masterpiece?

_____

_____

_____

_____

_____

_____

_____

_____

_____

_____

_____

_____

_____

_____

Even-tempered

The one who has knowledge uses words with restraint,
and whoever has understanding is even-tempered.
Proverbs 17:27 NIV

Restraint and even-tempered are not normally words that are used to describe me. Holding my tongue and patience are needed to achieve this. Knowledge and understanding come from studying the Bible. Sometimes we don't take the time to hold our tongue and wait for the knowledge in our use of words. I have to remind myself several times that people are not out to get me or do me wrong — including my kids — as I strive for understanding and an even-temper.

193

Loved

We love because He first loved us.
1 John 4:19 NIV

Once you accept the Lord as your Savior, He fills your heart overflowing with His love. And His love is so perfect and so complete that it doesn't matter if another living soul on the face of the earth loves you, because HIS love is all that you need. His love is steadfast and it never fails. And because His love is continuously poured out into you so perfectly, you are then free to love others and not expect anything in return.

Continue

Then Abram set out and continued toward the Negev.
Genesis 12:9 NIV

Following God is an exciting adventure! There is nothing like stepping out in faith when you feel called by God, but there are days when you start to doubt. Days when the answers don't come and the way is not as clear. Days when you want to turn and go back to your comfort zone. Be encouraged by Abram's example. You've done the hard part. You've set out... now, continue to walk by faith in what God has called you to do.

195

Stop

Listen to this, Job; stop and consider God's wonders.
Job 37:14 NIV

Read this verse again with your name in place of Job's. Our adversary
has won the battle when he can get us to focus on nothing but some
immediate concern. We all need to regularly stop and take in the
grandeur of God. From the vastness of the universe to the
precision of our DNA, God's majesty and purpose in creation
both diminishes our fears and reassures our heart of His control.
Of all God's wonders, you are who He gave Himself for.
Wake up with that thought every day.

196

Bruises

*We are hard-pressed on every side, yet not crushed; **we are**
perplexed, but not in despair; persecuted, but not forsaken;
struck down, but not destroyed—
2 Corinthians 4:8-9 NKJV*

It could always be worse! God is not in the business of saving our skin
at every brush with pain. He wants children who bruise, get up, and
keep going. Why? Because we have free will. We have to come to the
crossroads, armed and ready, laugh in the face of death, and know we
are indestructible when we are in Him.

197

Real Life

Think about the things of heaven, not the things of earth.
For you died to this life, and your real life is hidden with
Christ in God.
Colossians 3:2-3 NLT

When we ask Jesus into our hearts, our affections for the things of
this life slowly diminish. We die to our old lives and we are born to
our "real life" in Him. God will not fulfill all of His promises to us
in our temporary home. God will fulfill all of His promises to us in
our "real life" eternal home.

_____

_____

_____

_____

_____

_____

_____

_____

_____

_____

_____

_____

_____

_____

_____

_____

_____

_____

_____

Support

When I said, "My foot is slipping," Your love,
O LORD, supported me.
Psalm 94:18 NIV 1984

One second you are walking and the next you have hit some ice and you are going down. Despite your best efforts, you know you will soon be on the ground and hard. The same condition can hit you spiritually without warning. God knows. His love is your safety net; your climbing harness. God has not called you to a risk-free life. He calls you to exceed your comfort zone with the assurance He is your spotter. In today's terms, He has your back.

199

Cherished

For You created my inmost being;
You knit me together in my mother's womb.
Psalm 139:13 NIV

When you feel worthless, remember that God created you, individually, in His image, with love and detail like no one could or can. He created you with Love and in Love. And He is pleased with His creation, which is YOU. He is pleased with YOU. He cherishes YOU. He loves You like no other. Bask in His love and focus on it, blocking out all others because He is the only One who matters.

200

God's Gifts and Abundant Grace

But by the grace of God I am what I am, and His grace toward me was not in vain; but I labored more abundantly than they all, yet not I, but the grace of God which was with me.
1 Corinthians 15:10 NKJV

Where do your accolades come from? Whom do you credit for your accomplishments? Your family, your career, your education, your awards, and the praise you receive from others are all gifts from God. Yes we work hard, but it is by His grace alone that we are able to accomplish much. Don't lose sight of God's abundant grace poured into your life. Be careful not to become self-reliant in what God alone has allowed you to achieve.

201

Running

I run in the path of Your commands,
for You have set my heart free.
Psalm 119:32 NIV 1984

There are a number of life lessons in this verse. A path, by definition,
has boundaries: that's what makes it a path. When we trust through
faith that what lies outside the boundaries of the path is not spiritually
good for us, we can focus on running God's path without distractions.
Also, running on a path is easy. Running outside the path leads to
stumbling, bruises, or even losing your way completely:
all things that burden your heart and steal your joy.

202

Slow Fade

In the days when the judges ruled, there was a famine in the
land. So a man from Bethlehem in Judah,
together with his wife and two sons,
went to live for a while in the country of Moab.
Ruth 1:1 NIV

A famine doesn't happen overnight, and it seldom appears without
warning signs. Ruth moved to Moab during a famine, but I consider
the places I move to during a spiritual famine. I move away from the
Feast of the Word, away from the Living Water of Christ,
and into a dusty, dry existence where nothing grows.

203

Complete

The LORD is my strength and my shield;
my heart trusts in Him, and He helps me.
Psalm 28:7a NIV

I praise you because I am fearfully and wonderfully made.
Psalm 139:14a NIV

Complete! Hear it, dear one. You are complete in Christ.
He placed within you the gifts and talents needed to complete His
custom designed plan. Let go of the worry that you are inadequate.
Stop comparing. His power is sufficient. He will gently guide. Listen,
learn, look, see and follow. Your future is in His hands.
Do not despair. Find the joy in this day.

Why?

Have you not known? Have you not heard? The LORD is the everlasting God, the Creator of the ends of the earth. He does not faint or grow weary; His understanding is unsearchable. He gives power to the faint, and to him who has no might He increases strength.
Isaiah 40:28-29 ESV

The author's thought process in these verses is: The only reason anyone would not choose to follow God was they had not heard of or known Him. Why else would you not trust Someone everlasting, <u>the</u> Creator, tireless, with unsearchable wisdom, and compassionate to the weak? Why not trust Him?

_____

_____

_____

_____

_____

_____

_____

_____

_____

_____

_____

_____

_____

_____

_____

_____

_____

205

See Me

But if serving the LORD seems undesirable to you, then choose for yourselves this day whom you will serve, whether the gods your ancestors served beyond the Euphrates, or the gods of the Amorites, in whose land you are living. But as for me and my household, we will serve the LORD. Joshua 24:15 NIV

As Christians, we have a powerful means of testimony by providing physical evidence of our love of God. What differentiates our homes, cars, office, and clothes from that of a non-believer? What can we add to remind us and others of our devotion to Christ?

_____

_____

_____

_____

_____

_____

_____

_____

_____

_____

_____

_____

_____

_____

_____

_____

Refreshed

He makes me lie down in green pastures,
He leads me beside quiet waters, He refreshes my soul...
Psalm 23:2-3 NIV

We live in a world where imaginary hero badges are given for those with the busiest schedules. Buzzing smart phones, mile-long task lists and working around the clock have become commonplace. But God wants to give you the gift of rest. He longs to refresh and to restore your soul. Take a moment to ask Him how you can receive this rest in practical ways. Whether it's a ten-minute electronic break, or a walk in the park, be refreshed!

207

Created

For we are God's workmanship, created in Christ Jesus
to do good works,
which God prepared in advance for us to do.
Ephesians 2:10 NIV 1984

The Greek word used for workmanship in this verse connotes the idea of a masterpiece. A piece of art that is so good the creator desires it to be identified as his best! A creation, that when someone observes it, they immediately associate it with the creator. Keep all of this in mind should you ever question your worth. You are God's best, created with purpose, and intentionally given the talents you possess!

208

For Such a Time as This

*... if you remain silent... relief and deliverance will arise
... from another place... you and your father's house will
perish... have not attained royalty for such a time as this?*
Esther 4:14 NASB

How many times has my selfishness quenched His Spirit?
How often has fear of persecution or rejection silenced me?
WE CANNOT REMAIN SILENT! We must share what we have
witnessed and experienced through Jesus Christ, our Savior;
in such a way that His presence in, nor His love for the people of this
world could ever be denied.

_____

_____

_____

_____

_____

_____

_____

_____

_____

_____

_____

_____

_____

_____

_____

_____

_____

209

Sing

Rejoice in the LORD and be glad, you righteous;
sing, all you who are upright in heart!
Psalm 32:11 NIV

I've learned to sing in the midst of struggles. Once my family was in the middle of turmoil so I belted out, "It will be worth it all, when we see Jesus. Life's trials will seem so small, when we see Christ. One glimpse of His dear face, all sorrow will erase. So bravely run the race, 'til we see Christ." Immediately the clamor ceased and the room grew quiet. Singing calmed the storm.

Light

Blessed are those who have learned to acclaim You,
who walk in the light of Your presence, O LORD.
Psalm 89:15 NIV

God created the sun, moon and stars to govern the day and night and separate the light from the darkness. Likewise, His Spirit lives inside the hearts of believers to govern the good and shine through them to separate the good from the bad, not only the good and bad within us, but around us as well. Stop, focus on His ways and His commands, be still and know that He is in control. Be blessed by His presence.

_____
_____
_____
_____
_____
_____
_____
_____
_____
_____
_____
_____
_____
_____
_____
_____
_____
_____
_____

211

Enlightened

I pray also that the eyes of your heart may be enlightened in order that you may know the hope to which He has called you, the riches of His glorious inheritance in the saints, and His incomparably great power for us who believe.
Ephesians 1:18-19a NIV 1984

The word picture this verse paints is beautiful. Drink in these two undeniable truths with the eyes of your heart because that is where hope needs to be deeply rooted. As a saint, you share in the riches of His inheritance, and His incomparable great power which makes everything else possible!

212

Disposable

Man does not comprehend its worth;
it cannot be found in the land of the living.
Job 28:13 NIV 1984

It has been said that we are living in the "disposable age." We use things until we grow tired of them and then we either give them away, throw them away, or have a yard sale. Yard sale prices don't often reflect the true value of something just as our own sense of self worth is distorted. We pay a lot of money to look good and feel good, but invest little in the caring for our souls. We have been bought with a price and we belong to Jesus, body and soul. Let us live accordingly, filled with love and devotion for our Creator.

213

Conquerors

For I am convinced that neither death nor life, neither angels nor demons, neither the present nor the future, nor any powers, neither height nor depth, nor anything else in all creation, will be able to separate us from the love of God that is in Christ Jesus our Lord.
Romans 8:38-39 NIV

Paul went on to ask; who shall separate us from the love of Christ Jesus? The troubles of this world? Is it hardship, persecution, a failing economy, or danger? No, in the present troubles and heartaches we are more than conquerors through Him who loves us. Give Him praise today. No matter what… praise Him!

214

Generations

Your name, O LORD, is everlasting, Your remembrance,
O LORD, throughout all generations.
Psalm 135:13 NASB

The footsteps were evenly placed and deeply imprinted in the fresh tilled dirt. The earth smelled rich and clean. I carefully placed my little bare foot in each large footprint in the dark soil and left the outline of five wiggly toes just inside the bigger shape of Pawpaw's work boot. Step after uniform step, I followed Pawpaw as he plowed the garden. Oh LORD, as we follow You, let us leave behind worthy footprints of faith and good works. Help us to mark a clear path for the next generation to exalt Your name!

215

Comforted

Jesus wept.
John 11:35 NIV

Jesus came to earth as a man. He walked this earth
just as you and I, experiencing all the same emotions, troubles, joys,
and challenges. There is nothing that you will go through that He
did not experience, even the death of a dear friend. He understands
because He experienced it too. When you are sad, broken, lonely,
frustrated, or afraid, run to Jesus. Throw yourself at His feet and melt
into His arms. He understands and He will be there to comfort you.
He weeps with you.

216

Fearless

There is no fear in love. But perfect love drives out fear...
The one who fears is not made perfect in love.
1 John 4:18 NIV

When encountering fearful situations, only call on His name.
Believe in His Word and rest in His perfect love to drive out all fears
in order to conquer them; for we are more than conquerors
through His perfect love.

217

Continue

So then, just as you received Christ Jesus as Lord,
continue to live in Him,
Colossians 2:6 NIV 1984

The Christian walk can prove disheartening for new believers.
Once released from the bondage of sin it is discouraging to realize
temptations remain and stumbles are frequent. This verse contains the
simple remedy. As we received Christ, we should continue to live in
Him. When we receive Christ we are broken in spirit, convicted of
our need, and totally dependent on Jesus for redemption. To continue
living victoriously in Him requires the same three ingredients;
results in less of us, more of Him.

Renewal

You were taught, with regard to your former way of life,
to put off your old self, which is being corrupted by its
deceitful desires; to be made new in the attitude of your
minds; and to put on the new self,
created to be like God in true righteousness and holiness.
Ephesians 4:22-24 NIV

Every attitude we have, whether good or bad, is a reflection of God's righteousness and holiness in our lives. Are you drawing others to God or away from Him? Join me in praising God for daily renewal.

219

Rejoice!

Rejoice in the Lord always. I will say it again: Rejoice!
Philippians 4:4 NIV

In our Christian walk we go through many different seasons of life.
Some seasons are warm and sunny with new life abounding all around
us. Then there are the dreary cold rainy seasons when we want to
just pull up the covers and hide. Whatever season you are presently
walking in, you have one of two choices.
You can grumble and complain, "Woe is me!" or you can choose to
find something to rejoice about. Think of something the Lord has
done for you lately. Rejoice!

220

Wells

With joy you will draw water from the wells of salvation.
Isaiah 12:3 NIV

Digging a well in biblical days was a huge investment. There was the hard labor involved and the fact one's families and livestock depended on the well water's quality. Once determined to be good, a well became something to hand down through generations.

Think of the setback of completing a well to find the water was tainted. So it is today. Draw from the world's wells: emptiness and disillusion will be the reward. The bottomless well of God's salvation gushes with everlasting joy. Choose wisely!

221

Dance

God is sheer mercy and grace; not easily angered,
He's rich in love. He doesn't endlessly nag and scold,
nor hold grudges forever.
Psalm 103:8-9 MSG

Perhaps your mother or father became excessively angry when you
made mistakes. Maybe they constantly showed it with nagging and
repeated scolding. I'm so grateful for God's mercy and grace,
aren't you? Our Heavenly Father disciplines us with deep love.
Don't carry unnecessary guilt and shame.
Lay them down and dance in the fullness of His grace and love.

222

Mine

Do not fear, for I have redeemed you;
I have summoned you by name; you are Mine.
When you pass through the waters, I will be with you.
Isaiah 43:1b-2a NIV

We are never alone. Though we may feel as if we are, He is with us
passing through our circumstances. You are His. He says,
"I have called YOU by NAME." Sometimes as women, we need to
hear that we matter and we are noticed. God not only notices you,
He knows you individually. You are not lost in a diverse world.
You, *insert your name here* , are important to Him.

223

Everlasting

Before the mountains were born or You brought forth the
earth and the world, from everlasting to everlasting
You are God.
Psalm 90:2 NIV 1984

Do you ever wish there was just one thing in life that did not change?
Look to God. Given enough time, mountains erode. The sun's heat
changes in intensity. Even entire continents drift! God however, has
always been God. Nothing about Him has changed, nor will it. Ever!
Never-changing is a difficult idea to fathom but eternally comforting.
When you choose an anchor for your life, make it One that will hold
the same position forever!

Advance

Now I want you to know, brothers and sisters, that what has happened to me has actually served to advance the gospel.
Philippians 1:12 NIV

Everyone has a story. Whether your story has a happy or tragic ending, there is a purpose in it. I wonder if I can say, in the middle of my darkest days, that what has happened to me has advanced the gospel. Does your response to your struggle point people to Christ or does it make them wonder about your faith?

225

Weary

And let us not grow weary while doing good, for in due season we shall reap if we do not lose heart.
Galatians 6:9 NKJV

Doing good embodies detail—daily, unnoticed, uncelebrated, unappreciated detail. You let that car in at rush hour. You help that child with homework. You listen to that elderly neighbor tell you the same story, each time with more detail. We find ourselves weary, wondering, "What's the point?" The point: it is our purpose with a strong heart to do good, confident in our eternal celestial reward. This world cannot offer us such delight, so don't expect it to.

_____

_____

_____

_____

_____

_____

_____

_____

_____

_____

_____

_____

_____

_____

_____

_____

_____

Confession Leads to Healing

*Confess your sins to each other and
pray for each other so that you may be healed...*
James 5:16 NLT

We all need one or two mature believers to whom we can confess our
sins. We need to share our personal struggles, without the fear of being
condemned. We need to feel accepted for who we really are.
We need to be able to vent and trust our relationships will remain
intact. Confessing to other believers frees us from the chains of shame,
guilt, failure, and discouragement. It brings our sins out of hiding so
that Satan will not have strongholds on us.

_____

_____

_____

_____

_____

_____

_____

_____

_____

_____

_____

_____

_____

_____

_____

_____

_____

_____

_____

_____

Peaceful

Let the peace of Christ rule in your hearts, since as members
of one body you were called to peace. And be thankful.
Colossians 3:15 NIV

This verse implies two very important ideas. There are multiple
conditions that can rule our hearts and which one we allow is a
choice we make. Someone making the right choice is peaceful; full of
peace. Other descriptors include serene and calm. To meet someone
with this demeanor, you might describe them as Christ-like.
Life will certainly have its storms but even storms have their Master.
Choose the peace of Christ.

228

Do Not Compare

For a day in Your courts is better than a thousand.
I would rather be a doorkeeper in the house of my God
Than dwell in the tents of wickedness.
Psalm 84:10 NKJV

The enemy loves us to compare ourselves to others and breed
discontentment in our hearts. Be satisfied with the tasks God has
assigned you to do and thank Him for giving you the spiritual gifts
He has equipped you with.
One day at a task that God has assigned for you to do
is better than a thousand days trying to do someone else's job.

229

Walking the Talk

He has shown you, O mortal, what is good. And what does the LORD require of you? To act justly and to love mercy and to walk humbly with your God.
Micah 6:8 NIV

I often wonder how to be a "good" Christian and find myself wandering back to this verse. To act justly sounds easy enough… live a fair and honest life. Love mercy… showing kindness to those undeserving… that muddies the waters a little. And humble? That can be a tricky one. Good thing we are supposed to do all these things with our God. I couldn't do them alone.

Light

LORD... let the light of Your face shine on us.
Psalm 4:6 NIV

I wait in the quiet of a fresh new day basking in the wonder of creation. The sun peeking over the horizon lighting the sky is a reminder of God's faithfulness. His mercies are new every morning. Birds sing melodies of praise. Lush trees provide food, shelter and shade. This day God ordained unfolds before me. He is my Living Water; the sustenance of my soul. Fill me and spill me out to those in my presence, LORD. Let the light of Jesus shine in me.

_____

_____

_____

_____

231

Brokenness

The LORD is close to the brokenhearted and
saves those who are crushed in spirit.
Psalm 34:18 NIV

The one thing worse than being brokenhearted, is feeling guilty about
being brokenhearted. It can happen. Believers are supposed to be
joyful regardless of circumstances right? Yet the author of this Psalm
knew even with your full armor on, life can find a way to hurt you.
Life can crush your spirit; simply crush it! That is the time to cling to
this verse. At times like this, you need more than advice; you need a
Savior that is close. That's Jesus!

232

Reflection

Consider it pure joy, my brothers and sisters,
whenever you face trials of many kinds...
James 1:2 NIV

God, help us to glean the blessings from adversity in our lives. Give us the gift of perseverance, wisdom, and empathy while we focus on a season of reflection within the turmoil. Your promise is not to cause pain in this world, but to use it to restore and save others while growing Your kingdom. We pray we will view our circumstances, not as the world would, but with the clarity and compassion of Christ.

Our Life-Savior

... he became frightened... he cried out, "Lord, save me!"
Immediately Jesus... took hold of him...
Matthew 14:30-31 NASB

We are often spooked by darkness, and sometimes it's not the unseen
that terrifies us most, but the obvious, unavoidable danger that lies in
plain sight. And like Peter we cry out: "Lord, save me!" Immediately
He's there, rescuing us from the fear rising within.
We are never out of His reach! Seek shelter in the arms of God —
the source of undeniable peace and the place where weary and
frightened souls can truly find rest.

_____

_____

_____

_____

_____

_____

_____

_____

_____

_____

_____

_____

_____

_____

_____

Walking

...and by His light I walked through darkness!
Job 29:3b NIV

Although we seldom find ourselves in total darkness, it is an unnerving feeling when it happens. Your eyes are open and straining yet you cannot see. Groping blindly only leads to futility and frustration. Spiritually, darkness is every bit as debilitating. Knowing Christ is the polar opposite. There is irresistible brilliance and hope. Life becomes enticing. Even though you may be living in tough circumstances, your path is lit. No need to fear stumbling or going off course. No groping; you can walk with confidence in Him.

235

Interruptions

Therefore, as we have opportunity, let us do good to all people, especially to those who belong to the family of believers.
Galatians 6:10 NIV

Life is full of interruptions: telephones and doorbells ringing, children needing attention, unscheduled appointments, neighbors and friends stopping to chat. It is important to note that our Lord had more than His share of interruptions from both friends and enemies.
He still managed to complete the work He set out to do, all the while taking time to listen and help no matter how insignificant it seemed.
Oh, to be like Jesus. Help us, Lord, to see each interruption as an opportunity to be of service.

Genuine

These have come so that your faith — of greater worth than gold, which perishes even though refined by fire — may be proved genuine and may result in praise, glory and honor when Jesus Christ is revealed.
1 Peter 1:7 NIV 1984

Rejoice in your trials for your faith is being refined making you genuine for His use. Paul goes on to say; in this you are receiving the goal of your faith: the salvation of your soul in Christ Jesus.

237

Answers

Call to Me and I will answer you and tell you great and unsearchable things you do not know.
Jeremiah 33:3 NIV

One of the traits of Jesus that set Him apart in His ministry was the authority with which He spoke. People were in awe at the simple yet profound truths He taught. The fact we can have the same life teacher as Jesus often escapes us. God holds great and unsearchable (beyond our comprehension) truths; the path out of the maze; the key piece to the puzzle. Call to Him now, He loves to hear your voice.

_____

_____

_____

_____

_____

_____

_____

_____

_____

_____

_____

_____

_____

_____

_____

_____

_____

Heritage

For You have heard my vows, O God;
You have given me the heritage of those who fear Your name.
Psalm 61:5 NIV 1984

One of my earliest memories is going to church with my grandparents. I would lie on the hard, wooden pew tediously counting the tiles on the vaulted ceiling. There was comfort in a gentle hand touching my brow; peace as my grandmother's warbled soprano voice blended with the old baritone of my grandfather's. These recollections, mingled with many others, have left me a rich heritage. In the seemingly monotonous moments, may we endeavor to share love, to sing praise, and to pass on an inheritance of adoration for You, O God.

239

Accountable

For the word of God is living and active. Sharper than any double-edged sword, it penetrates even to dividing soul and spirit, joints and marrow; it judges the thoughts and attitudes of the heart. Nothing in all creation is hidden from God's sight. Everything is uncovered and laid bare before the eyes of Him to whom we must give account.
Hebrews 4:12-13 NIV 1984

I am so thankful that God gives us the ability to change our attitudes. When we focus on Him, our hearts are melted and we become like Him.

240

Empowered

I have given you authority to trample on snakes and scorpions and to overcome all the power of the enemy; nothing will harm you.
Luke 10:19 NIV

We have power in Jesus' holy name. We need not fear the enemy or his agents. Fear is a spirit that the enemy uses to decrease our effectiveness in the kingdom. But God has not given us a spirit of fear but power and authority. Take hold of the authority that you have in Jesus Christ and stand boldly against the enemy.
The Lord will always be with you.

241

Justified

Before this faith came, we were held prisoners by the law, locked up until faith should be revealed. So the law was put in charge to lead us to Christ that we might be justified by faith. Now that faith has come, we are no longer under the supervision of the law.
Galatians 3:23-25 NIV 1984

We were once slaves to sin being held captive by the law. The law revealed to us our need for Christ. We are now free, not because of any good works we have done but rather, because of what Christ did on the cross.

_____

_____

_____

_____

_____

_____

_____

_____

_____

_____

_____

_____

_____

_____

_____

_____

_____

_____

_____

Sunrise - Sunset

As high as heaven is over the earth,
so strong is His love to those who fear Him.
And as far as sunrise is from sunset,
He has separated us from our sins.
Psalm 103:11-12 MSG

How far is heaven above the earth? How far is sunrise from sunset?
We can't measure the distance. Neither can we measure His love,
grace and forgiveness. But we can choose to accept it
on bended knee with praise on our lips
and thanksgiving in our hearts.

_____

_____

_____

_____

_____

_____

_____

_____

_____

_____

_____

_____

_____

_____

_____

_____

_____

243

Walls

Break up your unplowed ground and
do not sow among thorns.
Jeremiah 4:3b NIV

Sometimes we do not allow God to dig up some of our fields. Those unplowed grounds are off limits. We say, "God, you can touch on anything you want to in order to grow me, but just don't go there." If I do go there and "break up my unplowed ground," I am also allowing God to remove my thorns of anger, resentment, victimizing myself, hatred, shame, a grudge, or denial. Will you allow God into your unplowed fields and remove the thorns?

244

Enduring

For everything that was written in the past was written to teach us, so that through endurance and the encouragement of the Scriptures we might have hope.
Romans 15:4 NIV 1984

Endurance is not a trait with which we are naturally born. Endurance is a learned characteristic of a survivor. Physical endurance is admirable but spiritual endurance is lifesaving. To endure there has to be motivation; a hope that makes a goal worthy of enduring a trial. That is where Scripture comes in: the stories, the victories, the overcomers who persisted through the storm and lived to celebrate the conquest encouraging us to do the same.

Whoyagonnacall?

... casting all your care upon Him, for He cares for you.
1 Peter 5:7 NKJV

Some days it feels like we do not matter. We have an insurmountable
"to do" list full of overdue items to make us feel that we have failed
from the moment we wake up. Who do we call? Mom? Sibling?
Make you feel any better? Of course not! How could they possibly
know what reaction you need—when you yourself don't even know?
What you need is to tell Him. He cares. He listens.
He loves you unconditionally.

Precious

Since you are precious and honored in my sight,
and because I love you...
Isaiah 43:4 NIV

We sometimes feel undeserving of love, especially when we have
been left so many times that we now believe we are not worth
staying for. We hold others at a distance for fear of abandonment.
If only we could see ourselves as our heavenly Father sees us.
He loves us like no one on this earth ever will or even can.
The best part is, He desires to spend eternity with us. We need not
fear being abandoned by God.

_____
_____
_____
_____
_____
_____
_____
_____
_____
_____
_____
_____
_____
_____
_____
_____
_____
_____

247

Calling

From the ends of the earth I call to You,
I call as my heart grows faint;
lead me to the rock that is higher than I.
Psalm 61:2 NIV

This Psalm clearly shows before we can ask for help we have to recognize the need for it. Any rock we stand on alone is not high enough. God loves us enough to allow us to get to the ends of our earthly attempts to discover that fact. When we are ready to be led, our hearts are ready for Him.

As we surrender our worst, we receive His best.

248

You Are the God Who Sees

Then she called the name of the Lord who spoke to her,
You-Are-the-God-Who-Sees; for she said,
"Have I also here seen Him who sees me?"
Genesis 16:13 NKJV

El-Roi, The God Who Sees Me, chose to manifest Himself to an
outcast maidservant in the desert. By a spring in the desert, He
sought her out and she became a believer in the God of Abraham.
Do you feel left out, abandoned, or alone? Maybe you are just
looking for a spring of water in the desert? El-Roi is here.
He sees You. He knows You. Pour out your heart to Him.

_____

_____

_____

_____

_____

_____

_____

_____

_____

_____

_____

_____

_____

_____

_____

_____

_____

249

We Can Do It! (Sort of!)

"Not by might nor by power, but by My Spirit,"
says the LORD.
Zechariah 4:6b NIV

I have this picture of Rosie the Riveter that hangs in my kitchen; she is the 1940's inspiration to women to maintain the war effort. The caption on the picture reads, "We can do it." I gave her a tattoo one day and wrote this verse on her bicep with a Sharpie. I tend to power through things on my own and forget that God needs to be the driving force.

What are you trying to muscle through on your own today?

_____

_____

_____

_____

_____

_____

_____

_____

_____

_____

_____

_____

_____

_____

_____

_____

_____

When

*When you pass through the waters, I will be with you;
and when you pass through the rivers, they will not sweep
over you. When you walk through the fire, you will not be
burned; the flames will not set you ablaze.*
Isaiah 43:2 NIV

Figuratively, trials can drown your spirit with anxiety and a feeling
of helplessness. Then there are times when life's challenges threaten
to parch your soul like a forest ravaged by flame. Either way, we are
goners except for His faithfulness. He is our buoyancy in deep waters
and our cool shelter in the firestorm.

_____

_____

_____

_____

_____

_____

_____

_____

_____

_____

_____

_____

_____

_____

_____

_____

_____

_____

_____

251

Wait

Wait for the LORD;
be strong and take heart and wait for the LORD.
Psalm 27:14 NIV

Waiting is difficult. Yet God's Word says wait, stand firm, and be patient. We must not go ahead, grab our circumstances and try to control the outcome. This is wearisome. Instead, sit still before the Lord, seek Him in His Word, tell Him your worries and listen. He gives peace. Our faith grows in the waiting. If we desire to behold God's righteous right hand, we must learn to watch and wait in wonder. His timing is not ours.

_____

_____

_____

_____

_____

_____

_____

_____

_____

_____

_____

_____

_____

_____

_____

_____

_____

_____

Wise Woman

Have I not commanded you? Be strong and courageous. Do not be afraid; do not be discouraged, for the LORD your God will be with you wherever you go.
Joshua 1:9 NIV

As God's daughters, we don't have to live in fear. There will certainly be times of trials, trouble, and even suffering in this world. God doesn't put these things in our lives, but He promises to use everything that happens for a positive, higher purpose. Take joy in that revelation and know He is always with you. Let the comfort of Christ whisper to you and offer courage!

253

Jesus Has Your Back

For I am confident... that He who began a good work in you will perfect it...
Philippians 1:6 NASB

Are you giving it your all, trying your best, and still feeling discouraged, disappointed and defeated? Come on brave girl! You've got this! Know why? Because you've got Jesus and nothing is too hard for Him. Ask Him to help you. The day you received His Holy Spirit is the very day the Father began a good work in you.
Rely on His strength! He will see it through. God never starts anything He can't finish.

_____

_____

_____

_____

_____

_____

_____

_____

_____

_____

_____

_____

_____

_____

_____

_____

_____

_____

Direction

Whether you turn to the right or to the left,
your ears will hear a voice behind you, saying,
"This is the way; walk in it."
Isaiah 30:21 NIV

Life presents us with so many opportunities to misstep and fear of a mistake can paralyze us. Should we slow down, speed up or change direction entirely? God has an intended path for each of us with directions available through His life atlas, the Bible. His counsel is of more worth than gold. With His word hidden in your heart, you will know immediately when someone gives you bad directions.

_____
_____
_____
_____
_____
_____
_____
_____
_____
_____
_____
_____
_____
_____
_____
_____
_____

Monsters in My Closet

Therefore, rid yourselves of all malice and all deceit,
hypocrisy, envy, and slander of every kind.
1 Peter 2:1 NIV

God was so clear about getting rid of things that represent the
'old self' and yet I sometimes find a piece tucked away.
Good intentions get tossed aside when a challenge comes and one of
these hidden creatures comes out to play. Do you find these monsters
in your closet too? It looks like effort is required on my part.
Today, I'm cleaning house, want to join me?

_____

_____

_____

_____

_____

_____

_____

_____

_____

_____

_____

_____

_____

_____

_____

_____

_____

_____

Love

Because Your love is better than life, my lips will glorify You.
Psalm 63:3 NIV

God's Word is the greatest love story ever written. Think of the love a
bride has for her husband. Now think of us as the bride of Christ and
His unconditional love for us. We were created for one purpose –
to have a loving relationship with God. Turn from pleasures
of the world and renew your commitment to God.
Draw near to Him and He will draw near to you.

_____

_____

_____

_____

_____

_____

_____

_____

_____

_____

_____

_____

_____

_____

_____

_____

_____

_____

_____

257

Safety

The wealth of the rich is their fortified city;
they imagine it an unscalable wall.
Proverbs 18:11 NIV 1984

Your safety is never in your finances, your home or your country.
Where do you look for your safety?
Your safety and security is in the Most High God!
Rest in knowing we serve a God that never slumbers!

Lover

On the third day there was a wedding in Cana of Galilee, and the mother of Jesus was there; and both Jesus and His disciples were invited to the wedding.
John 2:1-2 NASB

In Jesus' time, as in ours, weddings were a joyous time of celebration. What a romantic detail, to choose such a festive ceremony as a wedding for Jesus to perform His first miracle and to begin to reveal Himself and His character to us, His bride! Jesus was <u>invited</u> to this wedding. Maybe you've invited Jesus to be your Savior, your Forgiver of sins, but have you considered inviting Him to be your Bridegroom, the Lover of your soul?

_____

_____

_____

_____

_____

_____

_____

_____

_____

_____

_____

_____

_____

_____

_____

_____

_____

_____

Troubles

Though You have made me see troubles, many and bitter,
You will restore my life again; from the depths of the earth
You will again bring me up.
Psalm 71:20 NIV

Living the Christian life through Jesus does not bring an exemption
from trouble. Neither will it negate consequences from sin.
The author of this Psalm had seen many troubles, bitter, potentially
joy-killing tribulations. He also knew, not just hoped but knew his life
would be restored. Notice the author never says he understands the
reasoning, he just knows he will be raised up.
God's grace is always sufficient.

Commanded

A new command I give you: Love one another.
As I have loved you, so you must love one another.
John 13:34 NIV

The book of John tells us that we will be known by our love for each other. Only when we receive the love of Christ will we be able to love those around us completely and unconditionally. Take a moment to thank Jesus for His abounding, limitless and eternal love.

261

Confidence

This is the confidence we have in approaching God:
that if we ask anything according to His will, He hears us.
1 John 5:14 NIV

Because Jesus died for us and atoned for our sins, we can come to the
Father anytime we want and ask anything we want. He hears us.
He is not unapproachable, He is not scary, He is always available.
Pray that His will would be done in your life and never forget that
you can go to Him, anytime, anyplace and ask anything,
according to His will, and He will hear you.

Helper

In my alarm I said, "I am cut off from Your sight!"
Yet You heard my cry for mercy when I called to You for help.
Psalm 31:22 NIV

In the midst of troubling times we can feel like we've been hidden from God's sight. "He must have abandoned us," we think. It's when we call out to Him that we find that He's been there all along, waiting to help us. So don't delay any longer.
Call out to Him your Helper.

263

Prospered

From the time he put him in charge of his household and of all he owned, the LORD blessed the household of the Egyptian because of Joseph.
Genesis 39:5a NIV

Wait, did you catch that? Because one person sought God's face, the entire household of a very wicked person was blessed. Was that a comfort to Joseph? The text does not give us that answer but it should comfort us. God honors our struggles! Even when we feel as though our efforts are wasted, God is moving people's hearts.
Trust your circumstances to God and stand back.

Free

I run in the path of Your commands,
for You have set my heart free.
Psalm 119:32 NIV

When I was in high school, I ran track. My body, mind and soul
focused on one thing, running hard and running fast.
How exhilarating it is to run hard. How freeing it is to run as fast
as you can. Maybe you're like me and don't run as fast as you use to.
Even if we aren't able to physically run at all, we can and should run
hard and fast after Jesus through His Word.
He has set our hearts free!

Answering

Before they call I will answer;
while they are still speaking I will hear.
Isaiah 65:24 NIV

Have you ever picked up the phone to make a call only to discover
someone is already on it because you picked it up a moment before it
rang? That is the mental image this verse conveys. You can be at your
wit's end but before you can form a prayer, God not only knows,
He has the answer. You can search the world over;
you will never find someone who listens like God!
No interrupting, no feigned interest, no distractions.

_____

_____

_____

Restore

"But I will restore you to health and heal your wounds,"
declares the LORD, "because you are called an outcast,
Zion for whom no one cares."
Jeremiah 30:17 NIV

He cares. He loves you. He will heal your wounds. He will restore you
to health. If ever you feel as if no one cares, He DOES! Though you
may feel like an outcast, He will restore your thoughts and strength.
Praise Him! He will not let you go!

267

Silly

*You will keep **him** in perfect peace, **whose** mind **is** stayed on **You**, because he trusts in You.*
Isaiah 26:3 NKJV

How often throughout our day, do we think of God? Some days are more than others. Sometimes it takes a few inconveniences, startles or slow-downs to realize just how in control we are not! Then we look around, all the hustle and bustle surrounding us. We just have to laugh at how silly we must look before we catch a dose of reality! Peace comes with this perspective: He is in control.

_____

_____

_____

_____

_____

_____

_____

_____

_____

_____

_____

_____

_____

_____

_____

_____

_____

Truthful

Therefore, laying aside falsehood,
speak truth each one of you with his neighbor,
for we are members of one another.
Ephesians 4:25 NASB

In the Body of Christ, we should speak only the truth to one another
and never deceive one another. We are members of one body, with
one blood in Jesus Christ. One cannot deceive another without
deceiving one's self. When we lie to one another, we welcome
in the father of lies. The entire body is exposed and will become
contaminated if not cleansed promptly. Pray that we speak nothing but
the truth among us, concealing nothing from another member.

269

Guilty Pleasures?

... God, who richly provides us with everything
for our enjoyment.
1 Timothy 6:17 NIV

In a world where we can easily become saturated with the bad news
of the day, taking time to enjoy something, like a good book or a
bubble bath can feel frivolous... Like we aren't being "Christian"
enough if we aren't out crusading for a cause or trying to right a
wrong. Scripture tells us God has provided us with good things for
our enjoyment. So lose the guilt; take time to enjoy your life!

Waves

For I am the LORD your God, who churns up the sea
so that its waves roar — the LORD Almighty is His name.
Isaiah 51:15 NIV 1984

Ever wonder why you are drawn to the shore? What is it that is so
relaxing? What makes it so easy to fall asleep to the sound of the surf?
Yes, it is a wonderful place to be surrounded by His creation and time
seems to slow down but, by this Scripture, we are witness to a holy
choir that ceaselessly declares His mighty name.
What could be more comforting?

Her Hands

Above all else, guard your heart,
for everything you do flows from it.
Proverbs 4:23 NIV

One day, as I struggled with an extremely restrictive diet, I exclaimed
in frustration, "I don't look this way because I ate too much
asparagus!" Have you ever been there girlfriend? This verse from
Proverbs reminds us that our hearts are also reflective. When we allow
gossip, bad language, questionable ethics and garbage entertainment to
fill our thoughts… it ultimately finds our hearts. Yet when we guard
what we are exposed to with determination,
we protect our lives and those we touch each day.

_____

_____

_____

_____

_____

_____

_____

_____

_____

_____

_____

_____

_____

_____

_____

_____

_____

_____

Shhhhh... Listen... I Hear Him

*He who has an ear, let him hear what the Spirit
says to the churches.*
Revelation 3:6 NASB

Believer and non-believer, saved and unsaved, reach into your pockets,
take out your listening ears and put them on. Jesus requires your full
attention. Three times in this chapter Jesus is pleading with all those
who have ears to listen to what the Spirit, His Spirit, is saying. Can
you hear Him? He is speaking to you, pleading with you and
He wants your eyes, your ears and your hearts
focused on His every word.

273

Guided

Your Word is a lamp to my feet and a light for my path.
Psalm 119:105 NIV 1984

God teaches and guides you through His Word, the Bible.
Though He does not give it to you all at once, that would be too
overwhelming. Like a small flashlight in a completely dark forest,
He provides just enough light for you to see where to put your foot
next. All you need to do is believe that He is there and
trust that He is leading you in the right way.

274

Unexpected

For when You did awesome things that we did not expect,
You came down, and the mountains trembled before You.
Isaiah 64:3 NIV

I wonder why it is so easy to expect things from people, but we put
God in a box? We expect our husband to know what we are thinking,
our kids to know how to behave, our friends to know when we need
a listening ear, and yet we don't want to 'bother' God
with our daily needs. Today let's expect, anticipate and
hope for all the Lord wants to pour out!

275

Thoughts

You will keep in perfect peace all who trust in You,
all whose thoughts are fixed on You!
Isaiah 26:3 NLT

Be careful to see the clear cause-and-effect in this verse.
Who will be kept in perfect peace? All who trust in God.
Why are they able to trust? They trust because their thoughts are fixed
on God. The equation would be,
thoughts fixed on God = trust in God = perfect peace.
Peace is not a result of favorable circumstances.
Peace is a result of our thoughts being riveted on God.

Whatever

Finally, brothers, whatever is true, whatever is noble,
whatever is right, whatever is pure, whatever is lovely,
whatever is admirable — if anything is excellent
or praiseworthy — think about such things.
Philippians 4:8 NIV 1984

In this Scripture we are reminded of the choices to what we think about. Thinking about whatever is good and right is a skill all of us can learn. When a negative thought comes to our mind, we can make a tenacious effort to replace it with a positive thought. This will surely put a smile on God's face and ours too.

Remembered

Then those who feared the LORD talked with each other, and the LORD listened and heard. A scroll of remembrance was written in His presence concerning those who feared the LORD and honored His name.
Malachi 3:16 NIV

What do you want to be remembered for? Personal achievements, a big estate, high education…? Love, honor, fear, serve and be faithful to the LORD for He remembers those who talk and share of His goodness. Remember today the LORD is listening and His angels are recording!

278

Grace

But I have prayed for you, Simon, that your faith may not fail. And when you have turned back, strengthen your brothers.
Luke 22:32 NIV

Jesus knew that Peter would deny Him three times. And He knows that we will fail sometimes too. But take heart, He has prayed for you before the foundation of the earth that your faith will not fail. Run to Jesus when you sin and receive His love and forgiveness and then share your story with others so that you can strengthen and build them up as well.

279

Wind

... He walks upon the wings of the wind;
He makes the winds His messengers...
Psalm 104:3-4 NASB

When we moved to the very windy Texas panhandle, I began to
notice a strange habit developing in our 4 year old son within days
of our arrival. "Why do you keep putting your arms over your head
when we go outside, buddy?" I asked him. "I'm afraid the wind is
gonna blow away my hair!" I assured him that God had attached the
hair to his head with much more power than the wind could blow.
In fact, God is so powerful, He simply walks upon
the wings of the wind.

Hearts

I will give you a new heart and put a new spirit in you;
I will remove from you your heart of stone and give you a
heart of flesh. And I will put My Spirit in you and move
you to follow My decrees and be careful to keep My laws.
Ezekiel 36:26-27 NIV

God will never force us to heed His voice or coerce our obedience but
consider the clear choice between the results of our failed attempts and
His perfect plan for our lives. He offers a heart transplant that will save
our spiritual lives.

_____

_____

_____

_____

_____

_____

_____

_____

_____

_____

_____

_____

_____

_____

_____

_____

_____

_____

281

Tapestry

Jesus Christ is the same yesterday and today and forever.
Hebrews 13:8 NIV

A tapestry is an intricately woven piece of fabric with threads of
different colors and textures that create a masterpiece. God's Word
is a tapestry, a true masterpiece. When you delve into the study of
the Bible, you begin to realize how it is all woven together with
the "crimson thread of Jesus" running throughout from the Old
Testament to the New Testament; the same yesterday, today and
forever. Take regular time to study His Word. Allow God to speak to
you through it and create within you a masterpiece.

_____

_____

_____

_____

_____

_____

_____

_____

_____

_____

_____

_____

_____

_____

_____

_____

Singing

The LORD your God is with you, He is mighty to save.
He will take great delight in you, He will quiet you with His
love, He will rejoice over you with singing.
Zephaniah 3:17 NIV 1984

We are surrounded by a very noisy world and sometimes it is difficult
to think a single thought without distraction. God is singing over you
in delight! Let the Holy Spirit quiet you in this very loud world so
that you can hear the Father sing over you today.

283

Freedom

So you are no longer a slave, but a son;
and since you are a son, God has made you also an heir.
Galatians 4:7 NIV 1984

Does your life today reflect the rich inheritance we have in Christ?
Are you living the abundant life you were promised?
Take hold of Him dear one and LIVE!

284

Lover

If you love me, you will obey what I command.
John 14:15 NIV

God wants us to love Him. It is a matter of the heart.
God does not want us to follow rules to keep from getting into
trouble. He wants us to follow His laws because we love Him.
He wants us to understand that the rules are because He loves us, is
protecting us and keeping us safe. Nothing we do affects God's love
for us. We can neither gain His love nor diminish His love for us.
The same should be true of our love for Him.

285

Kindness

Be kind and compassionate to one another,
forgiving each other, just as in Christ
God forgave you.
Ephesians 4:32 NIV

God forgave you as a result of the sufferings of Christ.
He is an extremely kind and compassionate Savior. He forgave you
while you were still an enemy. When we think about this verse in that
context, how could we not forgive others? We are so thankful for His
forgiveness we want to show others the same
kindness and compassion.

Gathered

He tends His flock like a shepherd: He gathers the lambs in
His arms and carries them close to His heart;
He gently leads those that have young.
Isaiah 40:11 NIV

How specific is this description of God's love? His lambs are not
slung over the shoulder or tucked under an arm. They are gathered
and carried close to His heart. Something tells me this is the way He
prefers it: calming our runaway hearts, resting our weary legs while
carrying us to safety. Being the loving Shepherd He is;
He refuses to drive His flock. He gently leads.

287

Well-Watered

The LORD will guide you always; He will satisfy your
needs in a sun-scorched land and will strengthen your frame.
You will be like a well-watered garden,
like a spring whose waters never fail.
Isaiah 58:11 NIV

I love to stand back and admire my flower garden after a spring
shower. Drooping plants become fresh and vibrant.
God promises refreshment to us even in difficult times.
He will guide us, meet our needs, and strengthen us.
His Living Water never fails to refresh our thirsty hearts.

_____

_____

_____

_____

_____

_____

_____

_____

_____

_____

_____

_____

_____

_____

_____

_____

_____

Ah-Ha!

Call to Me and I will answer you and tell you great and unsearchable things you do not know.
Jeremiah 33:3 NIV

There is knowledge to be gained in the Bible. Seek Him and He will answer you with unsearchable things. Whenever you have an "ah-ha" moment when learning something new, think about getting that "ah-ha" from God. How much greater is that kind of wisdom and understanding?

289

Undeserving

Great peace have those who love Your law, and nothing
causes them to stumble.
Psalm 119:165 NKJV

God's law, above all, is to love. When we love His law we love to love.
It sounds simple, yet some people or situations are very difficult to
love. We stumble when we see flaws and judge them as undeserving
of love. By that standard, we also are undeserving. We must remember
when we walk straight with God we love, as freely as we are loved
ourselves, undeservingly.

Dwelling

One thing I ask of the LORD, this is what I seek: that I may dwell in the house of the LORD all the days of my life, to gaze upon the beauty of the LORD and to seek Him in His temple.
Psalm 27:4 NIV 1984

No matter the circumstances of our lives, be it our marital status, physical health, financial wealth or any other aspect; all else fades in comparison to dwelling in the house of the Lord. May we each day assign our spirits to gaze upon His beauty and seek Him in His temple.

_____

_____

_____

_____

_____

_____

_____

_____

_____

_____

_____

_____

_____

_____

_____

_____

_____

_____

_____

_____

291

Turn Away

Don't set foot on the path of the wicked; don't proceed in the
way of evil ones. Avoid it; don't travel on it.
Turn away from it, and pass it by.
Proverbs 4:14-15 HCSB

When God's Truth is revealed to us, we must start walking with
Him and His followers. One step with those we used to walk with,
will lead us back into the darkness. It is impossible to live according
to God's Word, while still exposed to our old way of life. All we can
do is pray for God to reveal His Truth to those we left behind.

292

Fashion Statement?

Let your light so shine...
Matthew 5:16 KJV

I am a walking advertisement for Christ: fish emblem and Christian
station bumper sticker on my car, t-shirts with Scripture on the back,
cross necklace. Clearly, I am a Christian. Everything about me says so.
But does it? If I put away all my trendy inspiration wear, would the
world still know? I love Jesus and want the world to know Him,
but sometimes I'm afraid I put Him between me and
the ones He came to save.

293

Trouble

I have told you these things, so that in Me you may have peace. In this world you will have trouble. But take heart! I have overcome the world.
John 16:33 NIV

We praise You for lifting us out of this sin-filled world that often provides trials. During difficult times help us to turn our eyes to You, accepting in full faith all the good You have in store for our todays and tomorrows. Let us turn our cares over to You and trust You to deliver peace to our hearts.

Overhaul

Therefore, if anyone is in Christ, he is a new creation;
the old has gone, the new has come!
2 Corinthians 5:17 NIV 1984

It is so tempting to hang on to the old stuff because it's comfortable.
We aren't ready for RADICAL CHANGE. We trick ourselves into
believing we can change a little at a time. Give that up? Eventually.
Stop doing that? Someday. Turn our back on the past? Later. The
Spirit encourages, counsels, convicts and changes. He wants to make
your life completely new. Are you ready for an overhaul?

Stars

He determines the number of the stars and
calls them each by name.
Psalm 147:4 NIV

Insignificant is not a word in our Lord's vocabulary. It has been
estimated there are a greater number of stars in the universe than
grains of sand on the earth. Not only that, their Creator calls them
each, yes, each, by name. The best estimates on the number of people's
names the average person can remember is 500 maximum.
Thus, another reason He alone is worthy of our worship.

Fear

The LORD Himself goes before you and will be with you;
He will never leave you nor forsake you.
Do not be afraid; do not be discouraged.
Deuteronomy 31:8 NIV

Fear is: False Evidence Appearing Real. Did you know that the
phrase, "Do not be afraid" appears 365 times in the Bible?
God wants us to know that we can depend on Him every day
of the year. Run to Him remembering that His perfect love
drives out fear.

_____

_____

_____

_____

_____

_____

_____

_____

_____

_____

_____

_____

_____

_____

_____

_____

_____

_____

297

Garments

I delight greatly in the LORD, my soul rejoices in my God. For He has clothed me with garments of salvation and arrayed me in a robe of righteousness, as a bridegroom adorns his head like a priest, and as a bride adorns herself with her jewels.
Isaiah 61:10 NIV

What are your favorite garments? Is it a festive gown, or an expensive coat or glamorous shoes? Nothing in this world can compare to the clothes we receive when we are born again in Christ Jesus. For He clothes us in His righteousness and when the Holy Father looks at us He sees the righteousness of His Son.

_____

_____

_____

_____

_____

_____

_____

_____

_____

_____

_____

_____

_____

_____

_____

_____

_____

298

Caring

Carry each other's burdens, and in this way
you will fulfill the law of Christ.
Galatians 6:2 NIV

Have you ever thought about how much easier the load is to carry
when we share it with one another? God created us for relationship
and is pleased when we carry our troubles to Him. He also desires for
us to love each other. Show someone how much you love them today
by offering to share their burden.

299

Patient

Love is patient, love is kind...
1 Corinthians 13:4 NIV

Jesus knows that we are not perfect and that we will sin and fall short
of the glory of God. So why do you expect perfection in yourself
and sometimes in others? We are forgiven sinners and Jesus loves us
unconditionally. His love is patient and kind. Patiently extend that love
to those around you and give and receive forgiveness as Jesus does.
Unconditionally.

The Eagle

Like an eagle that stirs up its nest, that hovers over its young, He spread His wings and caught them, He carried them on His pinions.
Deuteronomy 32:11 NASB

God will not allow us to become too comfortable in our relationship with Him. He "stirs up the nest" moving us from our comfort zone. This can ruffle our feathers and unnerve us until we remember that He is hovering over us and ready to catch and carry us should we fall. Keep your eyes on Him and fly!

301

Incarnation

Jesus wept.
John 11:35 NIV

It may seem at first that this verse contains little encouragement but the opposite is true. These two words and the situation that surrounds them are intimately revealing about who Jesus is. This is Deity displaying raw human emotion. While Christ was God in the flesh, He also understands our pain and the entire range of our sentiments. Family and friends may struggle to empathize, but Jesus' compassion is like no other. Open your heart to Him fully and know there is nothing that needs to be hidden.

Circumstances

Joshua son of Nun and Caleb son of Jephunneh, who
were among those who had explored the land, tore their
clothes and said to the entire Israelite assembly, "The land
we passed through and explored is exceedingly good. If the
LORD is pleased with us, He will lead us into that land,
a land flowing with milk and honey, and will give it to us.
Only do not rebel against the LORD. And do not be afraid
of the people of the land, because we will swallow them up.
Their protection is gone, but the LORD is with us.
Do not be afraid of them."
Numbers 14:6-9 NIV 1984

"Circum" means around and "stances" means standing, so circumstances
mean that you have obstacles or people standing around you that are in
your way. In this passage of Scripture Joshua reminds us to not look at our
circumstances but God's character. Only two of the twelve spies
saw something other than despair and hopelessness.
Trust in God's providence regardless of your circumstances and
God will lead you through your difficulties.

_____

_____

_____

_____

_____

_____

_____

_____

_____

303

_____

Sleep

I will lie down and sleep in peace, for You alone,
O LORD, make me dwell in safety.
Psalm 4:8 NIV 1984

Have you been sleepless lately? Have the troubles of this unstable
world burdened you so much that you have no peace? Carry all of
your troubles to the LORD for He cares for you!
He will give you His peace.

304

GPS

The road of right living bypasses evil;
watch your step and save your life.
Proverbs 16:17 MSG

"We live by the GPS. We die by the GPS," my husband stated emphatically as the dirt road we were travelling narrowed into a washed out gully. Dying by the GPS seemed the more obvious outcome as we ventured deeper into the backwoods, passing an intimidating house with a barking hound dog and a "POSTED. NO TRESPASSING." sign. Pursuing the GPS route, however, we found ourselves at the back entrance of a posh yacht club. Oh that I would resolutely stay the course, choosing God's Word as my GPS: God's Perfect Steps for me. He always bypasses evil and gives life!

_____
_____
_____
_____
_____
_____
_____
_____
_____
_____
_____
_____
_____
_____
_____
_____
_____

Censorship

Do not let any unwholesome talk come out of your mouths, but only what is helpful for building others up according to their needs, that it may benefit those who listen.
Ephesians 4:29 NIV

Words are powerful; especially when uttered aloud.
They can encourage a weary heart, or, all too often, rip someone to shreds. How well spoken are you? Ask the Holy Spirit to guide your speech and lift someone up today.

Refuge

I will say of the LORD, "He is my refuge and my fortress,
my God, in Whom I trust."
Psalm 91:2 NIV

Have you ever just wanted to run away and hide from the world?
The good news is that you do not have to run away to a dark corner
and hide. God is our refuge, our hiding place. He is an ever-present
help in times of trouble. He is always there and will never leave you or
forsake you. Rest in God, and don't hide, stand tall.
He will also be your shield and rampart.

_____

_____

_____

_____

_____

_____

_____

_____

_____

_____

_____

_____

_____

_____

_____

_____

_____

_____

Consolation

When anxiety was great within me,
Your consolation brought joy to my soul.
Psalm 94:19 NIV 1984

The Latin root of the word "console" means intensive comfort. Isn't that God's style? When someone needs comforting, He provides it intensively. The author of the Psalm testifies to that very quality. His anxiety was great; all consuming. God's comfort did not simply quiet his soul. It took his emotional state to the opposite end of the scale. No one else can provide that for us. Horizontal relationships are no substitute for a vertical relationship with our Creator.
From gloom to glee, He is able.

308

Speak-up

But in your hearts set apart Christ as Lord. Always be
prepared to give an answer to everyone who asks you to give
the reason for the hope that you have.
But do this with gentleness and respect.
1 Peter 3:15 NIV 1984

Do you want to be encouraged dear one? Ask the Lord to help you to
speak up and share your faith today with others. You never know what
God is doing in and through you. Study the Word and be prepared
through prayer and always share the Good News in a gentle and
loving way. There is a dying world right next door to you,
so go and speak-up in His love. No matter what,
you will rejoice in doing your Father's will!

309

Messenger

Do everything without complaining or arguing,
so that you may become blameless and pure, children of God
without fault in a crooked and depraved generation,
in which you shine like stars in the universe as you hold out
the word of life—in order that I may boast on the day of
Christ that I did not run or labor for nothing.
Philippians 2:14-16 NIV 1984

Jesus set the perfect example of how we are to live.
Though we are undeserving of the honor, He entrusts us to carry
His message to the world. Does your life point others to Christ?

310

All-Powerful

When a strong man, fully armed, guards his own house, his possessions are safe. But when someone stronger attacks and overpowers him, he takes away the armor in which the man trusted and divides up the spoils.
Luke 11:21-22 NIV 1984

No matter how strong the devil may be – Jesus will always be stronger. For by Him all things were created. Jesus has already won the battle. No one is stronger than Jesus!
Put your trust in Him and Him alone.

Goodness

Give thanks to the Lord, for He is good.
His love endures forever.
Psalm 136:1 NIV

Everything God does is good. Maybe you're in a place that has you
wondering if any good can come from it. Do you know and believe
that God sees and understands? His faithful love will last forever.
It is never ending. Give Him thanks today for His goodness
and His faithful love.

_____

_____

_____

_____

_____

_____

_____

_____

_____

_____

_____

_____

_____

_____

_____

_____

_____

_____

_____

Watch

But as for me, I watch in hope for the LORD,
I wait for God my Savior; my God will hear me.
Micah 7:7 NIV

Have you ever watched a pot of water boil? You sit in anticipation,
knowing that the little bubbles will slowly rise to the top of the
surface. You KNOW because it has happened before. Why is it so hard
for us to remember that God will hear us every time we pray?
We need to watch and wait in anticipation, just like the water, because
we KNOW that every time we call He WILL hear us.

313

Temporary

*For His anger **is but for** a moment, His favor **is for** life;*
*weeping may endure for a night, but joy **comes** in the morning.*
Psalm 30:5 NKJV

There will be trials, and there will be tears, for every living thing.
We cannot build a life, a home, a family that is prepared enough
to prevent, nor strong enough to withstand, all pain. Suffering is
simply part of this life. The ever-present lesson is to realize the pain is
temporary. God's deliverance is permanent.

314

Set Your Mind

Set your mind on things above, not on earthly things.
Colossians 3:2 NIV

The wisdom of today's verse would seem to defy common sense.
Life brings certain responsibilities about which we all need to have
some level of concern in order to provide for ourselves and for those
in our care. We get our priorities twisted when we depend on those
things for our contentment, allowing the attainment of them to
control us, causing anxiety in our hearts. God's intention is for us to
devote our thoughts and ambitions toward the things of His kingdom.
In them is true peace and ultimate satisfaction.

315

Rested

Come to me, all you who are weary and burdened,
and I will give you rest.
Matthew 11:28 NIV

We live in a demanding world, full of deadlines and expectations.
We try to keep up with it all and do our very best.
Oftentimes we become weary and burdened by expectations.
When you become weary, stop, find a quiet place and open your
Bible. Jesus is there waiting to renew and refresh your soul. He is there
to give you rest. Allow His words of peace to wash over you like a
gentle rain and let go of your burdens.

316

Planted

*Now the LORD God had planted a garden in the east,
in Eden; and there He put the man He had formed.*
Genesis 2:8 NIV

Do you ever feel out of place? At times I've wondered,
"What on earth am I doing here?" But the truth is, God carefully
places us in the perfect spot to encourage our growth.
Take comfort knowing the Master Gardener planted you
right where you are on purpose.

Crying

"Woman," He said, "why are you crying?
Who is it you are looking for?"
John 20:15a NIV 1984

He has risen! Let His resurrection pour into your life today. Look no
more because His power can resurrect anything! Do you have a dead
marriage that needs His resurrection power or a dying relationship
with a child or family member? Put away crying and remember to
look to Jesus! Let His power work in your situation today.
Do not lose heart for He cares for you.

318

Power

Some trust in chariots and some in horses,
but we trust in the name of the LORD our God.
Psalm 20:7 NIV

This verse contains the two most common methods people use to battle circumstances bigger than themselves. Some fight (chariots) and some try to escape (horses) but neither choice is successful all the time. Only those who trust in the name of the LORD will endure every time. The Author of life also has the ultimate power in life. He will provide your spiritual sustenance, your determination, your rescue, and your peace. His Name will provide all you need.

319

Aliens

But our citizenship is in heaven. And we eagerly await a Savior from there, the Lord Jesus Christ, who, by the power that enables Him to bring everything under His control, will transform our lowly bodies so that they will be like His glorious body.
Philippians 3:20-21 NIV

God has promised to redeem this broken world. He created perfection and sin brought destruction. In these dark days, hold fast to the hope we have in Jesus and the glorious homecoming He's prepared for His children.

_____

_____

_____

_____

_____

_____

_____

_____

_____

_____

_____

_____

_____

_____

_____

_____

_____

_____

Sing

Let the godly sing for joy to the LORD;
it is fitting for the pure to praise Him.
Psalm 33:1 NLT

I love birds and I love the old hymn, "His Eye Is On The Sparrow".
Even more than that, I love that God mentioned birds in Scripture.
We could learn a lot from a sparrow. When it is under attack from
an enemy, it sings! When difficult times surround you, sing praises to
God. I can't promise that the difficult times will be removed,
but I can promise a change in your heart.

_____

_____

_____

_____

_____

_____

_____

_____

_____

_____

_____

_____

_____

_____

_____

_____

_____

Floodgates

"Bring the whole tithe into the storehouse, that there may be food in My house. Test Me in this," says the LORD Almighty, "and see if I will not throw open the floodgates of heaven and pour out so much blessing that there will not be room enough to store it."
Malachi 3:10 NIV

Test the Lord on this one. God was not kidding about His eye being on the sparrow. My husband and I have four children.
Being a stay-at-home, homeschooling momma, we have one income.
We have never been in need. Test Him; He is good on His word!

Ouch

If any of you lacks wisdom, let him ask of God, who gives to all liberally and without reproach, and it will be given to him.
James 1:5 NKJV

We gain wisdom through observance and experience. Like little children, we must accept the "ouch" moments on the road to wisdom and realize it is a gift. The greater the lesson, the more likely it will involve pain. So let us ask for the tools and talents we seek, and earnestly follow God through to them.

323

Peacekeeper

What is causing the quarrels and fights among you?
...You want what you don't have... you are jealous of what
others have, but you can't get it, so you fight...
to take it away from them...
James 4:1-2 NLT

We want what others have. We want to do the things others do.
We want to be like those of whom we think so highly.
Jealousy says, "God owes me." Reality is God owes us nothing!
God created us for His purposes, not our own. Praise God for who
you are and for everything you have. Be a peacekeeper.

_____

_____

_____

_____

_____

_____

_____

_____

_____

_____

_____

_____

_____

_____

_____

_____

_____

_____

Unfailing Love

"Though the mountains be shaken and the hills be removed,
yet My unfailing love for you will not be shaken nor My
covenant of peace be removed," says the LORD,
who has compassion on you.
Isaiah 54:10 NIV

There is literally nothing we can lean on that is unfailing, except
God's love. His compassion draws us to Him; His understanding of
our condition penetrates our pride, exposes our frailty.
Even though there is such upheaval that everything around us is
collapsing, His love remains. God's heart is in His covenant with us,
there is no chance of it being removed.

325

Refreshed

*Take My yoke upon you and learn from Me, for I am gentle
and humble in heart, and you will find rest for your souls.
For My yoke is easy and My burden is light.
Matthew 11:29-30 NIV*

Jesus offers to share our burdens. He does not desire that we be
weighed down by them. He does not promise us a life of ease and
comfort. He promises that He will always be with us.
He will help us carry those burdens if we partner with Him by
spending time with Him.
Learn from Him. Rest in His shadow and be refreshed.

326

Affirmation

Do not let any unwholesome talk come out of your mouths,
butonly what is helpful for building others up according to
their needs, that it may benefit those who listen.
Ephesians 4:29 NIV

We all have one thing in common, relationships. We don't need people
to treat us the way we deserve. No, deep inside we long for others to
treat us with the same care as our Savior, with love and grace.
Today find words of affirmation that will build up, benefit and make
an eternal impact on others.

_____

_____

_____

_____

_____

_____

_____

_____

_____

_____

_____

_____

_____

_____

_____

_____

_____

327

Magnified

I will praise the name of God with song and
magnify Him with thanksgiving.
Psalm 69:30 NASB

This verse is built on the precept that the closer we examine or
magnify God, the greater will be our appreciation of Him. Just as
we can, with time, take loved ones for granted, we can also become
accustomed to living in God's grace. When we set aside time to
consider His place in our lives our souls respond with thanksgiving,
humility blossoms and troubles diminish. Praise creates an upward
spiral. The greater magnified He is, the more in awe we become.

328

Believe

They replied, "Believe in the Lord Jesus, and you will be saved—you and your household."
Acts 16:31 NIV

Are you praying for a loved one to come to the Lord and be saved?
Keep praying. Be encouraged for this is the will of our Father, that no
one should perish but that all should come to repentance.
Do not lose heart; continue to pray for them.

Wait

Wait for the LORD; be strong, and let your heart take courage; yes, wait for the LORD.
Psalm 27:14 NASB

A friend congratulated my daughter on her recent high school graduation. He asked her how she felt about completing this season of her life. She responded, "Now that I'm finally here, I don't know what to do with myself." How often do we run around so busily trying to accomplish a goal, only to find ourselves at a loss for what to do next when we've finished! Sometimes we must wait, gather our courage, and wait some more while we seek God's will for the next season of our life.

Value

So then, just as you received Christ Jesus as Lord,
continue to live in Him, rooted and built up in Him,
strengthened in the faith as you were taught, and overflowing
with thankfulness. See to it that no one takes you captive
through hollow and deceptive philosophy,
which depends on human tradition and the basic principles of
this world rather than on Christ.
Colossians 2:6-8 NIV 1984

Oh sweet one: never, ever fall victim to the lies of this world.
You are priceless. You are His.

_____

_____

_____

_____

_____

_____

_____

_____

_____

_____

_____

_____

_____

_____

_____

_____

_____

_____

331

Transformed

*And do not be conformed to this world, but be transformed by the renewing of your mind, that you may prove what **is** that good and acceptable and perfect will of God.*
Romans 12:2 NKJV

The false glitter and sparkle of this world constantly threatens to distract us from our wholehearted devotion to Christ. When we obey the Holy Spirit's promptings to focus on Christ, our minds are renewed and we draw closer to His sweet presence.
The result is a life that glitters and sparkles for Him.

Bread

Jesus answered, "It is written: 'Man shall not live on bread alone, but on every word that comes from the mouth of God.'"
Matthew 4:4 NIV

In China, many dedicated Christians are arrested every day just for reading and practicing Christianity. If caught, their section of the Bible will surely be confiscated and they will be thrown into jail and used for slave labor. All of them know this cost, but the price is worth every word that comes out of the mouth of God.
Do we live off of the Word?

333

Rulers

He who is slow to anger is better than the mighty,
and he who rules his spirit than he who takes a city.
Proverbs 16:32 NKJV

Power is not impressive to God. Why should it be? We can fake it all
we want—manipulate the masses and conquer by force. God watches,
hardly amused, His little children playing "King of the Hill," awaiting
the patient sigh of the wise child, the one who knows he is limited
and has accepted his humanity. God values our incapacity—He made
us that way! We don't have to prove anything to Him.

Deep Water

When He had finished speaking, He said to Simon,
"Put out into deep water, and let down the nets for a catch."
Luke 5:4 NIV

We often find ourselves in a similar circumstance involving our faith.
Sometimes God's direction just defies what our already failed efforts
have proven; yet, He asks us to trust Him and put out into deep water.
The world says to repeat the same actions and expect a different result
is the definition of insanity, true when the actions are self-directed.
When the directions are from God, it is called faith.
To not listen is insanity.

335

Cultivating

Very early in the morning, while it was still dark,
Jesus got up, left the house and went off to a solitary place,
where He prayed.
Mark 1:35 NIV

Jesus is our example. He shows us how to live our lives.
He spent time with the Father each day, praying, and having a
personal relationship. God desires a close relationship with us as well.
Nothing else is as important as our relationship with Christ.
Try not to get so caught up in ministry, or doing good,
that you neglect times of solitude with the Father.

More

But you are a chosen people, a royal priesthood,
a holy nation, God's special possession, that you may declare
the praises of Him who called you out of darkness
into His wonderful light.
1 Peter 2:9 NIV

You are more. You are more than numbers on a scale. More than the price tag on your clothes. You are more than the number of likes on Facebook or followers on Twitter. You are smart, funny, kind, beautiful and worthy of love. You are so priceless that someone gave up His life for you. Inhabit your worth.

337

Assurance

... that their hearts may be encouraged, being knit together in love, and attaining to all riches of the full assurance of understanding, to the knowledge of the mystery of God, both of the Father and of Christ...
Colossians 2:2 NKJV

Rejoice in full assurance of your salvation in Christ Jesus. For if you know the Son, you know the Father for They are One. Don't let the troubles of this world bring you down today. Be encouraged in your salvation, in Jesus! He lives and now you are alive in Him.

338

Expectation

My soul, wait silently for God alone,
for my expectation is from Him.
Psalm 62:5 NKJV

This verse identifies a key characteristic of a person whose anchor
is God. The author's expectation is from God. No matter the
circumstances, this person knows he will hear from God. Just as the
sun will rise each morning, God's unmistakable involvement in the
believer's life is assured. Expectation is stronger than hope because
it's based on experience. Expectation is faith fully matured.
God will surely keep His promise of hearing our prayers.
His answers are perfectly timed and suited to each of us.
Ask Him to help you be quiet and listen.

339

Lovely

A new command I give you: Love one another. As I have loved you, so you must love one another. By this all men will know that you are My disciples, if you love one another.
John 13:34-35 NIV 1984

Are you known by your love for others? Most days I don't feel like I am, but Jesus commanded us to love one another: even the unlovable. Take a moment and ask God to remind you how much He loves you, then show that love to others so they know whose you are.

_____

_____

_____

_____

_____

_____

_____

_____

_____

_____

_____

_____

_____

_____

_____

_____

_____

_____

Humbled

*For His anger lasts only a moment, but His favor lasts a
lifetime; weeping may stay for the night,
but rejoicing comes in the morning.*
Psalm 30:5 NIV

God knows we battle our sin nature every day. We don't always win.
We sin. We fall. We mess up. But God is a good God; understanding,
faithful, compassionate, and full of mercy and grace. He will discipline
us and then, He will pick us up, dust us off, hug us, and send us back
out to try again. When you miss the mark;
confess, repent, and get up and try again.

341

Honesty

*God **is** Spirit, and those who worship*
Him must worship in spirit and truth.
John 4:24 NKJV

Exhaustion, trials and suffering cause our feelings to go haywire.
Often we are ashamed of our honest thoughts and attitudes. We think,
I'm a Christian, I shouldn't think or feel this way; so we try to hide
them from God, silly isn't it? He knows us better than we know
ourselves! Prayer is the best place to reveal our true feelings. Honesty
in prayer is a safeguard against acting on our own feelings.

_____

_____

_____

_____

_____

_____

_____

_____

_____

_____

_____

_____

_____

_____

_____

_____

_____

_____

_____

Hope Well Placed

And so, Lord, where do I put my hope?
My only hope is in You.
Psalm 39:7 NLT

Today's verse could have been written by King Solomon after he had
reached the end of his life and reflected on his pursuit of wisdom,
worldly gain and contentment. For all the lavish material possessions
he gained, he realized none of it brought peace to him.
Likewise, if our hope is anchored to anything other than God,
it will prove to be only temporary and false when put to the test.
Only in the steadfastness of God will our hope flourish.

Spoiled

How great is the love the Father has lavished on us, that we
should be called children of God! And that is what we are!
The reason the world does not know us
is that it did not know Him.
1 John 3:1 NIV 1984

The word spoiled has many meanings, doesn't it? Food can spoil; we
can spoil our life to ruin, or raise spoiled rotten children. However,
as believers in Christ Jesus we have been spoiled by the Father in a
different way. We have been loved by the Father and He has lavished
His love on us, while we were still in our sin, He sent His Son to die
in our place! Be encouraged today for you have been spoiled by the
Most High God!

344

Fearless

The LORD is my light and my salvation—
whom shall I fear?
The LORD is the stronghold of my life—
of whom shall I be afraid?
Psalm 27:1 NIV

Fear is ungodly. No matter what the circumstance, we are told not to fear. Many times I find myself believing the deception Satan whispers in my ear: you're not good enough, you don't matter, you can't do that... horrible, ugly lies! Commit Psalm 27:1 to memory and shout it aloud when fearful thoughts enter into your head.
Whom then shall we fear since we are not alone?

345

The Shield of Faith

So do not throw away your confidence;
it will be richly rewarded.
Hebrews 10:35 NIV

In ancient Greece, one of the great dishonors of battle was for a warrior to lose his shield to the enemy. This meant to surrender the most important part of his defense and was practically a death sentence. Paul exhorts us to not lay down our faith (our confidence or shield) in the face of spiritual adversity. That exposes us to the enemy. Moreover, if we persevere, the victory is that much sweeter and our reward is a faith that is even stronger.

346

Bread

Jesus answered, "It is written: 'Man shall not live on bread alone, but on every word that comes from the mouth of God.'"
Matthew 4:4 NIV

In China, many dedicated Christians are arrested every day just for reading and practicing Christianity. If caught, their section of the Bible will surely be confiscated and they will be thrown into jail and used for slave labor. All of them know this cost, but the price is worth every word that comes out of the mouth of God.
Do we live off of the Word?

347

Voice

*Your ears shall hear a word behind you, saying, "This **is** the way, walk in it," whenever you turn to the right hand or whenever you turn to the left.*
Isaiah 30:21 NKJV

Trusting that voice is easier said than done. It's a constant struggle to balance our carnal instincts and our moral compass. Still, the main ingredient to hearing this voice is: stilling your soul, opening your mind, and listening. God is directing us toward good—the word is behind us—we just need to listen.

_____

_____

_____

_____

_____

_____

_____

_____

_____

_____

_____

_____

_____

_____

_____

_____

_____

_____

_____

_____

_____

_____

348

Not Alone

*But when He, the Spirit of truth, comes, He will guide you
into all the truth... He will tell you what is yet to come.
John 16:13 NIV*

The Holy Spirit is our Advocate, Faithful Guide, Defender,
Helper, Comforter, Counselor, Teacher, and Friend. Which one of
these do you need Him to be for you today? Have you invited Jesus
Christ to be your Lord and Savior? If not, do it today, don't wait.
He is waiting to be all these things to you. If Jesus Christ is your Lord,
ask Him to be that which you need Him to be today.

349

Suffering Comforted

My comfort in my suffering is this:
Your promise preserves my life.
Psalm 119:50 NIV

The word used for "comfort" in today's verse appears in only one
more Old Testament book, Job. It is meant to convey the type of
comfort that is unique to the deepest kind of affliction.
Even when life was bleakest, God's promises provided rays of hope in
the darkness. That promise is there for us also. Never will He desert
you, reject you, disown you, or walk away from you.
He knows your suffering and is there to carry you through it.

350

Investment

Do not store up for yourselves treasures on earth, where moth and rust destroy, and where thieves break in and steal. But store up for yourselves treasures in heaven, where moth and rust do not destroy, and where thieves do not break in and steal. For where your treasure is, there your heart will be also.
Matthew 6:19-21 NIV 1984

Truly valuable possessions are things we can never purchase on our own. Christ paid the ultimate price for our eternal salvation when He died in our place.
Have you given Him a good return on His investment in you?

_____

_____

_____

_____

_____

_____

_____

_____

_____

_____

_____

_____

_____

_____

_____

_____

351

Prayer

*Listen to my voice in the morning, LORD. Each morning
I bring my requests to You and wait expectantly.*
Psalm 5:3 NLT

God delights in your presence. He desires that you engage in
conversation with Him about the daily stuff of life. Don't worry about
"proper" words in prayer, just talk to Him. Share your hurts, share
your sorrows, and share your joys. Share your heart freely and honestly.
God listens intently in love and compassion.

Overwhelming Love

Fear and trembling have beset me;
horror has overwhelmed me.
Psalm 55:5 NIV

King David's life was filled with extremes. He experienced victories
unlike many others but also knew the feeling of trepidation for his
life while being pursued by enemies. His successes were extraordinary,
his failures devastating. The lesson we should extract is the source of
David's recovery. When it comes to dealing with life we have choices.
We can be overwhelmed by the uncertainty, the injustice and
sometimes the horror. Or we can be overwhelmed by God's love,
set free by His mercy, and transformed by His grace.

353

Delight

Delight yourself also in the LORD,
and He shall give you the desires of your heart.
Psalm 37:4 NKJV

Let's play word association: Delight. Pleasure. Indulgence. Chocolate. Gooey. Calories! Diet. Exercise. Sweat. Water. Replenish. Sound about right? We delight ourselves in things that feel good. Seemingly against our nature, we are admonished to delight ourselves in God—not ourselves—in order to fulfill our deepest desires. Why? Because where God's love is at work, so are His blessings flowing. (And the aftermath still ends in "Replenish"—without the nasty "Diet"!)

From the Inside Out

And you also were included in Christ when you heard the Word of truth, the gospel of your salvation. Having believed, you were marked in Him with a seal, the promised Holy Spirit, who is a deposit guaranteeing our inheritance until the redemption of those who are God's possession—
to the praise of His glory.
Ephesians 1:13-14 NIV

Christ is the Rock of our salvation. We are marked and set aside as special. We are heirs to the throne of Jesus Christ. We belong to God. He will never forsake us. The Holy Spirit is transforming us from the inside out. What is more important; rules or love?
Love trumps all.

_____

_____

_____

_____

_____

_____

_____

_____

_____

_____

_____

_____

_____

_____

_____

_____

Going for God

Now go; I will help you speak and
will teach you what to say.
Exodus 4:12 NIV

This was the message from God to Moses to meet with Pharaoh about releasing the Israelites. Some translations use the phrase "I will be with your mouth" to describe how God was going to specify the words of Moses. God did not provide a script to read to Pharaoh. He wanted Moses to arrange the meeting and trust God would then supernaturally orchestrate the rest. We see that in our lives also. When we have faith and follow His direction, miraculous things happen.

Guidance

Only be careful, and watch yourselves closely so that you do not forget the things your eyes have seen or let them slip from your heart as long as you live. Teach them to your children and to their children after them.
Deuteronomy 4:9 NIV 1984

Sometimes I find myself relying on outside sources for guidance and forget to listen to the internal source of wisdom God gave me: the Holy Spirit. I've also been known to forget that God's Word will guide me as well. Take a moment to reflect on how well you seek His guidance.

Loved

Then Jesus asked them, "Which is lawful on the Sabbath: to do good or to do evil, to save life or to kill?"
Mark 3:4a NIV

Rules are important. They keep us safe, and provide structure and discipline. God IS LOVE. His greatest commandment to us is to love Him and love others. He loves all of His creation. He is full of compassion. Living life in black and white is shallow living on the surface. Dig down to the nitty gritty. Take the risk to feel and love. What is more important; rules or love? Love trumps all.

Listening

The LORD came and stood there, calling as at other times,
"Samuel! Samuel!" Then Samuel said,
"Speak, for Your servant is listening."
1 Samuel 3:10 NIV

Have you ever met someone who talked nonstop? Talking and asking questions but rarely taking the time to listen to your answers? Frustrating and annoying isn't it? I wonder if God puts His holy chin in the palm of His holy hand and lets out a long sigh as we talk and talk, ask and ask, but rarely take time to listen to Him.

God's Voice

... but the LORD was not in the wind; and after the wind an earthquake, but the LORD was not in the earthquake; and after the earthquake a fire, but the LORD was not in the fire; and after the fire, a still small voice.
1 Kings 19:11-12 NKJV

God's voice can only be heard if you are where you can hear God. It is not only about your physical location, it is about your "heart" location. Are you willing to listen and obey? He may answer in an unexpected way, but God will speak. Keep praying until you hear from Him.

His Name

No king is saved by the size of his army;
no warrior escapes by his great strength.
Psalm 33:16 NIV

It is natural to develop a false sense of security based on the things
of the world. We find ourselves self-assured if our profession is stable,
finances are in order, and the doctor praised our last physical.
There is no fault in rejoicing in blessings, but remove all the
accumulations in our life, and we should still have the praise of
Jehovah Jireh on our lips. There is nothing more capable of providing
fulfillment to our souls than His name.

Vessel

Jesus said to them, "A prophet is not without honor except in his own town, among his relatives and in his own home."
Mark 6:4 NIV

You don't need to be respected or honored to be used by God.
Don't let the rejection of your friends, neighbors, or family keep you
from serving God. Keep doing good. Don't give up the good fight.
Cling to Jesus and keep your eyes on Him.
He will work through you to bring glory to the Father.

Ask

...You don't have what you want because you don't ask God for it... even when you ask, you don't get it because your motives are all wrong—you want only what will give you pleasure.
James 4:2-3 NLT

We can't always get what we want. But God wants us to ask Him anyway, knowing He is the source of all good things. He wants us to come to Him for everything. For our own good, we won't receive things that feed our cravings and desires.
He wants to be the only object of our affection.

_____
_____
_____
_____
_____
_____
_____
_____
_____
_____
_____
_____
_____
_____
_____
_____
_____
_____

363

Doer

You are the light of the world. A City on a hill cannot be hidden. Neither do people light a lamp and put it under a bowl. Instead they put it on its stand in the house. In the same way, let your light shine before others, that they may see your good deeds and praise your Father in heaven.
Matthew 5:14-16 NIV

Witnessing is not about your words or your deeds. It is about bringing honor and glory to God. Be a doer of the Word, not just a speaker. Life is not at all about YOU. It is all about God.

364

Good is Jehovah

Good is Jehovah for a strong place in a day of distress.
Nahum 1:7a YLT

Nahum refers to a day of distress, but it is not unusual for distress to settle in for a season. That is precisely why it is good to have a strong place like Jehovah instead of a temporary shelter.
A brief shower can be endured in any old lean-to but a howling hurricane requires something (or Someone) that is anchored.
You might say His sheltering is tailored to us as individuals.
Although most of life is not within our control, good is Jehovah!

365